Guided by Whales

By Rebecca Pillsbury

Guided by Whales

Cover Design by Antonio Garcia Martin

Published by Duende Press

ISBN: 978-0-9915254-2-3

To all animals in captivity, everywhere

TABLE OF CONTENTS

SECTION VI: THE WEB OF LIFE

CONCLUSION: THE INTERCONNECTEDNESS OF ALL THINGS

RESOURCES

ECO-FRIENDLY LIFESTYLE TIPS

INTRODUCTION

In many Northwest Coast Native cultures, it is believed that whales have access to all the information that exists in the universe. To come into contact with them—even to catch sight of one—is considered an omen portending acquisition of vast spiritual powers. The whale is revered as a guide that leads to the discovery of the meaning of one's own life.

Not everyone's perception of cetaceans is as climactic. But for those who are fortunate enough to have spent time with these powerful creatures of the sea, it cannot be denied that there is something extraordinary about them. By virtue of their sheer size, the abundance of life energy they possess is greater than that of any other creature; their physical presence, therefore, is something we not only see but most likely feel.

It's a feeling that is universally difficult to describe. Even as a writer, I find that words completely fail me. All I know is, similar to others featured in this book, the whales called out to me. Energetically, emotionally, spiritually—something inside of them reached out to something inside of me and said, *Come along*.

The ways in which I responded to that calling have mostly been subtle and difficult to isolate. I could say I was touched by their beauty and intrigue ever since I saw orcas in the movie *Free Willy* at the age of eleven. I was living in Wisconsin and had never seen the ocean, but suddenly I knew I had to be close to it. After college, I moved to Oregon and made as many trips to the coast as I could.

My first time seeing those majestic mammals in the wild was alongside my parents, who were visiting. Fittingly, a female killer whale was resting with a calf beside a rock off Ecola State Park (the park itself is named after the Chinook word for *whale*). They were quite a distance away, but my excitement could not be contained. I screamed. Even from afar, they were stunning.

I wanted more, but I felt I lacked the educational background to get any closer—to be out on the water with the whales, daily if possible, which would require earning money while doing so. I had flirted with the idea of studying marine biology in college, but when I saw all the chemistry and physics classes I'd have to take, I turned toward what felt safer for my right-brained being, communication studies.

I went on to pursue various careers over the following years, including owning a petsitting business. I'd always loved animals, and that was one way to get paid for being around them. But the dilemma always nagged—what I loved more than anything were really big animals. Those that weighed anywhere from 400 pounds to 150 tons, for example. Hardly house pets.

After the visit with my parents, my next notable experience seeing whales in the wild came after enrolling in a volunteer program through Oregon State Parks called Whale Watching Spoken Here. After attending the two-day training, volunteers are stationed at lookout points along the coast during peak gray whale migration periods. I was there to answer questions and help visitors spot whales—though I had never seen a gray whale myself! About halfway through that first day, I did, however. This time, I cried.

I was reminded of that calling—come along. That whisper that every time I came closer became louder and more profound. It would not be ignored, try as life might to suppress it. I did learn that it could be quieted. It became like a seed lying dormant for the winter, waiting for me to shine some light on it.

I finally did, when I realized I did not need to have an academic science background to immerse myself in the topic. I could do what I already did: write. After publishing my first book in 2014 and even before publishing a subsequent book in 2016, I knew what the topic of my third book would be about. I had to write about whales.

However, it turned out that the book I'd had in mind to write had already been written. *Of Orcas and Men: What Killer Whales Can Teach Us* faced me down in a bookstore in Bellingham, Washington. I bought that book, and it was beautiful. Way better than I could have written, I admitted. So, what angle would I take with my book now? I wondered. I already had a plethora of research I'd conducted that could be repurposed in many different ways.

While attending the Marine Naturalist Training Program through the Whale Museum in Friday Harbor, Washington in 2017, I answered that question. Numerous participants stood up and declared their reason for being there: "I wanted to become a marine biologist so I could study whales, but I didn't want to take all those science classes.

There were so many people just like me in this regard—not wanting to channel our passion for whales through formal study but through environmental protection and lifelong learning. I could write a book for us.

The more I read during the research process, the more I realized how interconnected everything is—not just the ecosystem but our effects on it. People in every career could help protect the whales. In other words, we don't have to be marine biologists.

Cetacean field research is a pretty demanding lifestyle that requires time away from family, fierce competition for funding, extremely uncomfortable conditions, and potentially unrelenting sea sickness. If that is what you want, then by all means, go forth, my friends, and become marine biologists. But most people have other callings in life that are even greater.

This book follows the journeys of twenty-two people whose lives have been "guided by whales" but not necessarily ruled by them. Through artistic, political, educational, and yes, scientific endeavors, they heeded an inner calling to do something about the precarious state cetaceans are in, that state existing mostly as the result of thoughtless human behavior.

This book seeks to demonstrate how many different paths can be taken to answer the same calling I myself felt from the whales. We don't have to be scientists—in fact, what the world needs as much as scientists are people who can touch human hearts and perhaps encourage change in human thought and behavior.

Individual and collective action is needed more than ever to ensure a future where whales—and even our own species—can exist. The survival of us both depends on the existence of a habitable planet. And right now, we humans aren't doing so well with keeping our earth and our oceans sustainable.

Here are just a few of the critical threats facing cetaceans today that are explored in this book:

- Habitat degradation
- Prey depletion
- Entanglement in fishing gear
- Ship strikes
- Toxic contamination
- Oil and gas development
- Whaling
- Captivity
- Climate change

These concerns and what can be done about them are woven within personal stories, since I believe personal story to be one of the best ways to inspire, educate, and motivate individuals. If these people can make a difference, why can't we? Note that the Pacific Northwest is an epicenter for conservation efforts and cetacean sightings (and the region in which I myself reside), so it is generously represented among these stories.

Here are the inspirational stories of artists, filmmakers, educators, naturalists, nonprofit administrators, and researchers and biologists too. Here also are the stories of members of Indigenous cultures whose tribes have been guided by whales since well before European contact created so many of the problems cetaceans face today.

In many Native coastal cultures, it is believed that whales have access to all of the information that exists in the universe. If we listen to what they have to teach us, if we respond to that whisper—come along; follow me—we may be surprised as to what we discover.

I
BIOLOGY, SOCIOLOGY, AND INTELLIGENCE

At some point, every human ponders the essence of what it means to be alive. *Who am I? Where did I come from? What is the meaning of life? What is my greater purpose?*

To come to a conclusion regarding any of those questions, a considerable amount of time for study or reflection is required. Before modernization, moments of leisure were hard to come by—basic requirements of survival consumed our time and energy. Now that everything from electricity to dishwashers to meal delivery services has become normalized, we have enough time to mull over existential questions.

Except, we don't. We tend to fill newly acquired space in our lives with other personal, social, and work pursuits. It makes me wonder what we're missing. Just as much, it makes me wonder what other creatures, who have not allowed themselves to be trapped by technology and convenience, aren't missing—what they have figured out. Here with us on earth, there are mammals that have been evolving for over 50 million years, as opposed to modern man's two hundred thousand years. Members of that same order possess brains that are up to seven times larger than ours. Surely, those mammals have figured something out about life that we haven't yet.

American novelist Cormac McCarthy suggested in his unpublished screenplay *Whales and Men* that the enormous mind of the whale possesses the key to understanding creation. After all, some whale species go for months without eating; others have no natural predators and thus require no expenditure of energy to escape. Some have been known to live over one hundred years.

What do they do with all that time? What do they process with those enormous brains?

John Lilly, a neuroscientist and writer who explored human consciousness and dolphin communication, believed it likely that they contemplate the universe. McCarthy fantasized that to be true. In his play, he envisioned God returning to earth to ask humans if they've figured out they could pose their existential questions to the whale. In a twist, God then looks about and asks where the whales have gone.

If McCarthy's and Lilly's suppositions are true—and our planet loses this valuable resource to extinction—our own species could be left posing existential questions for all of eternity. We probably will anyway, but nevertheless, it is compelling to consider that we have in our great oceans—at least for now—a remarkably aware species that has survived first on land and later in the sea for millions of years. Ask anyone who has looked into the eye of a whale, and they will tell you that its depth reaches far beyond what can be seen in any other animal or human form.

These are species with biology, sociological structures, and intelligence so highly advanced that it's impossible to fully grasp just how exceptional these characteristics are. They are species that spend their lives submerged in a substance within which we cannot survive. Nevertheless, we try our best to understand them with the tools we have available to us.

Much of what we know about whales and dolphins today comes from observing them in the wild, in captivity, and in the flesh—by performing necropsies on carcasses that have washed ashore. In order for us to better absorb the topics that will be addressed later in this book, I offer some background information on the biology and sociology of this book's three most commonly discussed species of cetaceans: orcas, humpback whales, and gray whales.

More research has been conducted on orcas than on many other cetacean species, due to their accessibility. Some of the wild members of this species frequent areas in close proximity to humans. Their smaller size and sociability means they are easier to capture and hold in captivity, where they are further studied. So, please note that their attributes are discussed in this book more than some other species of cetaceans—though knowing more about the rest would undoubtedly prove to be equally fascinating.

Biology of Cetaceans

Whales, dolphins, and porpoises are believed to have descended from land animals that returned to the water roughly 50 million years ago after having lived on land. These marine mammals compose the order of Cetacea, which consists of around ninety different species of animals. Cetaceans can further be broken down as either toothed whales (i.e., sperm whales, beaked whales, beluga whales, dolphins, and porpoises) or baleen whales (i.e., gray, humpback, blue, minke, fin, and bowhead whales).

Most toothed whales are smaller than baleen whales but eat larger prey (such as fish, squid, seals, sea lions, and even other members of the cetacean order); their sleeker and smaller shape makes them faster and therefore better hunters. Instead of teeth, baleen whales have plates with bristles attached to their upper jaws, which are used to filter their food in the water; they eat small prey such as fish, krill, and plankton.

Aside from size and how and what they eat, differences between toothed whales and baleen whales include how they breathe, communicate with each other, and socialize. Toothed whales breathe through only one blowhole, while baleen whales have two blowholes (their blow appears to be heart-shaped, if viewed from in front or behind).

Breathing is conscious for both toothed and baleen whales. Only one half of their brain shuts down while they sleep, while the other half stays on the lookout for predators and obstacles and remembers to surface to breathe. After about two hours, the sides of the brain reverse, and the rested half awakens. Curiously, humpback and sperm whales have also been witnessed sleeping while hanging vertically, with their tails or noses poking out of the water.

To communicate, toothed whales use their blowhole to create high-pitched clicking and whistling sounds. They also rely on echolocation (the reflection of sound) to locate food, avoid predators, and navigate in the dark ocean. Toothed whales are expert stalkers who rarely vocalize while hunting.

Baleen whales communicate by producing loud, deep, low-pitched moans that can be heard from miles away; they are not dependent on echolocation as are their toothed counterparts. Interestingly, both species of cetaceans react to our music (when played live, not as a recording), since it resembles their own mode of communication. It is a phenomenon first described by the ancient Greeks.

Toothed whales tend to have more sophisticated social structures than baleen whales, partly because they require working together in order to hunt larger prey. Many whale pods, or social groups, have established social hierarchies and can be seen playing games together and teaching each other survival strategies. Certain cetaceans demonstrate their own cultures that are not unlike human cultures; they develop close relationships with family and friends and even mourn the deaths of members of their social families.

Social Lives of Orcas

Some of the more incredible examples that illustrate what make orcas (used interchangeably with their common name of killer whale) both different from and similar to humans are found in their social lives. When a killer whale gives birth, one or more adult "midwives" help the newborn to the surface to take its first breath. Orca society is strongly matriarchal; both female and male offspring stay with mom's family group for life. This social structure permits older whales to teach younger whales their territorial landmarks and the location and timing of their available prey.

The amygdala, or the part of the brain that's associated with emotional learning and long-term memories, is highly developed in orcas—suggesting that they could be retaining intergenerational memories. In fact, it has been observed that the orcas of the Puget Sound waters near Seattle, Washington, do not return to places where members of their families were captured—not even those who were born after the captures occurred go there.

For such a social animal, an abundance of empathy is mandatory; the whale brain has therefore evolved to expand this emotional trait, and the animals have learned to use it to their advantage. After a successful hunt, they share the food. Males have been observed leaving the best fishing holes for females and babies. Healthy whales have been seen supporting injured or sick whales.

Theirs is a culture based on cooperation; there are hierarchies of dominance, led by the matriarchs, but there's little sign of competition. When the Resident orcas of the Salish Sea (the network of coastal waterways that includes the southwestern portion of British Columbia, Canada, and the northwestern portion of Washington State) encounter other family groups and create a superpod, they display a ritual greeting ceremony to express their elation and joy.

Resident (fish-eating) and Transient (mammal-eating) orcas, although very rarely violent toward each other, do not mingle or interbreed. They have their own communication calls and cultural behaviors and more or less respect each other's territorial zones. Perhaps these mammals coexist peacefully because they live in transparency; their highly evolved sonar allows them to detect not only physical conditions (such as cancer, tumors, and strokes) but emotional states in each other. They can "see" inside of each other (and humans!) by transmitting sound waves. If a male orca wanted to compete with another male for a female, the interested parties would be able to determine the winner in advance simply by sensing each other's physical capabilities and emotional states—no fight needed.

What a whale assesses through the use of echolocation is also shared; if an orca mother transmits a sound wave, the results of that transmission are heard by her baby and other orcas in the vicinity. There are no secrets in orca society. Astonishingly, the amount of information they receive through sending a sound wave is twenty times the amount of information humans can receive with their hearing (which is also more than humans can perceive through vision—the primary sense for most of us).

Perhaps even more astounding is the ability of certain species of whales to instantaneously convey an image to each other—an orca can send an image of a fish to another orca hundreds of miles away, for example. This begs the question, if they can read each other's minds as well as see inside a human's physical body, can they also read human minds? Further, can they pick up on the energy of humans and even of objects?

Passengers on a Washington State ferry were in awe in the fall of 2013 when the vessel was surrounded by nearly three dozen orcas who appeared to be joyously celebrating. It was a spectacular event within itself but was made even more magnificent since the ferry was carrying five hundred ancient artifacts of the Suquamish Tribe. After fighting for decades to get these artifacts back on their land, the tribe rejoiced as the relics made their way from a museum in Seattle. The orcas seemed to be rejoicing too.

Orcas have been interwoven into the Suquamish tribe's cultural and spiritual practices since ancient times. Were the orcas able to pick up on the energy of the artifacts? Or the celebration in the thoughts of the tribe members? Or the spiritual significance of the artifacts on board?

No matter if they can read our minds and emotional states or not, it cannot be denied that whales possess a powerful sense of empathy not only for each other but for humans. Orcas are unique among apex predators (predator at the top of the food chain) in that they do not harm life forms they choose not to eat. Lucky for us, despite the many reasons we have given them to go against their makeup and harm us, they have agreed not to eat us. Perhaps it's their large amygdala that's responsible for their colossal ability to forgive. For whatever reason, they have decided we are worth sparing—and sometimes even establishing friendships with.

There have been several cases in which orcas have initiated contact with humans in an effort to play; they have a sense of humor and cleverness that rivals their human counterparts'. Some people even report orcas working in collaboration with humans; Australian whalers had a history of killing baleen whales and leaving the lips and tongues for the orcas to enjoy before collecting the rest of the remains. In what appeared to be an exchange, the orcas would protect the whalers when they were endangered by sharks.

The Kwakiutl tribe of the Pacific Northwest Coast maintains stories of how killer whales have saved their people from drowning or shown them where to find food in times of famine. Many Native coastal tribes consider it taboo to harm an orca; it is widely believed that if people kill an orca, the orca's family will seek revenge the next time the humans are out on the water.

Orcas are considered by many Native peoples to be not just our friends but our ancestors—loved ones whose spirits have returned to live under the sea. It is common to see killer whales carved into totem poles and family crests—the animal's spirit is foremost in power and prestige.

Social Lives of Humpback Whales

In general, humpback whales are solitary creatures that prefer traveling alone or in small groups of two or three. However, several dozen whales may come together to cooperatively meet their biological needs of hunting, migrating, and mating.

A pod may consist solely of a mother whale and her child or one or two friends who have formed a temporary loose bond. Friendships between female humpbacks have been witnessed, however, such that the same females reunite multiple years in a row during the summer breeding season. Interestingly, those that had the most stable relationships gave birth to the most calves.

Humpbacks embark on one of the longest migration routes of any species; they are known to travel as far as sixteen thousand miles from their summer cold-water feeding grounds to their winter warm-water breeding grounds. Mature whales have been witnessed traveling ahead of the younger whales, leading them to their established migration destinations.

Humpback whales have a unique bubble-net feeding technique where a group of whales circles prey, blowing bubbles to herd the school of fish into a tight ball. Loud vocal sounds are also used to scare the fish to the water's surface, after which the whales slap their fins against the water to stun the fish. Once the fish are immobilized, the whales swim up and lunge at them with open mouths. They take in hundreds of thousands of small fish with each gulp; they filter the meal through their baleen bristles (made of keratin, the same substance as human fingernails) to avoid digesting water.

During mating season, humpback whales rarely (if at all) feed; they live off the blubber (fat) reserves acquired during the feeding season, which allows them to focus on the more pressing task at hand. An extraordinary display of acrobatics (breaching, lunging, and tail slapping) accompanies mating season and is believed to be a method of communication that demonstrates male dominance and physical prowess. Charging at other males is another way to win a female mate, although it is rare that serious harm is inflicted.

In contrast to using aggression, there are populations of male humpback whales who are notably gentle and known as the singers. Their sound is created by pushing air out of the blowhole. Each "song" can last over twenty minutes, the "concert" can continue for more than twenty-four hours, and this "music" can be heard many miles away. Whales that are miles apart sometimes harmonize; they have even been known to change their songs already in progress to be in harmony with other whales.

Since these songs are performed by groups of males during mating season, scientists suspect the melodic vocalizations have something to do with attracting a mate. Their mating songs can sometimes be misunderstood by human ears to be the moans and whines made when the whales lose a friend or family member or feel lonely, but those are different sounds that also demonstrate their ability to feel emotion and empathy.

The only known predators to hunt humpback whales are orcas, which also cooperatively hunt baby gray whales. Orcas are rarely successful in carrying out a humpback kill, however, as humpback whales are considerably larger. In contrast, humpback whales are known as the sea's protectors and have been seen aiding not just members of their own species who are in danger but members of multiple other species. There are hundreds of recorded incidents of humpbacks coming to the aid of gray whale calves, seals, sea lions, and porpoises being hunted by orcas.

One humpback whale was even filmed protecting a human diver who was at the mercy of a tiger shark. Biologist Nan Hauser was diving off the Cook Islands in the South Pacific in September 2017 when the shark started stalking her. The humpback approached and guided her out of harm's way, first tucking her under its pectoral fin and then lifting her out of the water onto its back. Perhaps such apparent acts of altruism are why humpback whales earned the nickname "gentle giants."

Social Lives of Gray Whales

Like humpback whales, gray whales typically travel alone or in small, fluid groups. Associations among individuals mostly consist of mother-calf pairs. However, they may form larger groups when on feeding and breeding grounds.

Gray whales are one of the primary cetaceans contributing to the whale watching industry. Their predictable, near-shore migration route—alongside humpback whales, the longest of any species—makes them easy marks, as does their annual breeding routine in the lagoons of Baja California, Mexico. Before they were whale watching icons, however, they were heavily targeted by whalers for their oil.

Initially, gray whales existed in three distinct populations: Eastern North Pacific, Western North Pacific, and North Atlantic. The latter became the first and so far only whale species driven to extinction. The remaining populations are protected species, and hunting them is illegal.

The Eastern North Pacific population has recovered from near extinction to the point where, in 1995, it became the first whale to be removed from the United States' endangered species list. Today, an estimated twenty thousand gray whales make up the population, which is approximately equal to pre-whaling estimates. The Western Pacific population, however, has not recovered from whaling and is believed to be close to extinction.

One of the contributing factors to the recovery of the Eastern North Pacific gray whale (also known as the California gray whale) could be that they are the only baleen whales to feed mainly on bottom-dwelling organisms—therefore, they have little competition for food. As bottom-feeders, the whales hunt by swimming to the bottom of the ocean, turning on their sides, scooping up sediments that contain small organism prey, and filtering out the water through their baleen plates. An adult gray whale eats approximately two thousand four hundred pounds of food per day while in its summer feeding grounds.

Another possible reason for their ability to repopulate is their migration pattern, which makes it easy to encounter potential mates. Every October, small groups of Eastern North Pacific gray whales make their way from feeding grounds in the Bering and Chukchi Seas to the southern Gulf of California and the Baja California Peninsula of Mexico, where they mate and give birth. The migration takes an average of two to three months to complete, as they travel throughout the day and night for a total of up to nearly fourteen thousand miles.

Gray whales choose shallow waters to give birth, which is a practice believed to help prevent their calves from being attacked by killer whales, which are the only known predator of gray whales, aside from illegal human poachers and hunters. Despite the latter, the gray whale–human relationship has pretty much done a one-eighty since the days of commercial hunting. The whale was nicknamed "devilfish" by whalers, due to its aggressive nature and tendency to fight back when it felt threatened. Today, a thriving whale watching industry exists in the very birthing lagoons in Mexico where they were nearly driven to extinction.

Although people are allowed to touch gray whales in Mexico (it is illegal in United States waters), the whale watching industry in Mexico is highly regulated and known for its ethical policies and practices. The number of boats that can be out on the water at any given time is restricted, as are the areas boats can enter. No boats can enter the southern inlet or upper lagoon of San Ignacio Lagoon, where calves are nurtured. In addition, boats must maintain a particular distance from the whales; if passengers are able to touch the whales, it is because the whales came to the boat on their own accord.

About 10 percent of the whales in the Baja Peninsula birthing lagoons are what have been dubbed "friendlies." These whales regularly approach boats, allowing themselves to be pet and kissed by eager and enthusiastic humans. Some mothers even nudge their calves up to the boats, as if teaching them to inspect this curious other species. The whale's ability to trust humans is quite remarkable, as many of the whales that return to the lagoons are old enough to remember having been hunted in the area. One particularly popular whale, known as Scarback (gray whales have been photo identified and cataloged according to unique physical features), even bears the wound of a harpoon—but remains one of the friendlies.

Whereas humpback males can show aggression when competing for females, gray whales practice cooperative sharing of the females. There are even reports of male gray whales taking turns supporting the female while she copulated with another male. Perhaps that practice is another reason the California gray whale has managed to recover after being heavily hunted! Once sexually mature, female gray whales spend 80 percent of their lives pregnant or lactating. Unlike the endangered and highly toxic Southern Resident killer whales that frequent the waters of the Salish Sea, gray whale calves have a good chance of surviving past infancy.

The Most Intelligent Species on Earth

Although all cetaceans demonstrate unique aspects of intelligence, the species that has captured the most interest among the public is the orca, or killer whale. The name *killer whale* is a misnomer in more ways than one. Orcas are members of the dolphin family and are not killers in terms of exhibiting aggression or attacks on humans. Basque whalers witnessed orcas killing baleen whales and labeled them *ballenas asesinas*, "whale killers." The name was mistranslated into English and is still popularly used.

The orca species can be broken down into four distinct populations that look nearly identical but are genetically, behaviorally, and culturally different. The Southern Resident killer whale population is perhaps the most beloved and well-studied of all orca communities, due to their proximity to human activity. This population summers in the waters of the southern Salish Sea around British Columbia and Washington and winters as far south as Central California.

The Northern Resident killer whale population also frequents the Salish Sea, although primarily resides farther north than the Southern Residents. The Transient killer whale population passes through the same region but does not tend to stay for long as their geographic territory extends as far as from Alaska to California. Finally, there are the Offshore killer whales, of whom little is known, as they travel so far out to sea that human contact and observation are extremely limited.

Orcas are believed to have the second-largest and second-heaviest brains of any mammal, after sperm whales (some contest that an adult orca brain is larger than a sperm whale brain). Size isn't necessarily indicative of intelligence, but it's also worth noting that the killer whale's cerebral cortex is much more convoluted than the human cortex. This suggests a complex brain, driven by the social intricacy and highly communicative lifestyle of these top predators of the ocean. Baleen whales, which do not have to socialize and hunt for their food, do not have brains as large as toothed whales, although their size and structure also suggest a high level of complexity.

What We Can Learn from Whales

We humans tend to perceive all animals as less intelligent than ourselves because they do not think or communicate like humans. However, if we open our minds to the possibility that our species is limited by our own brain's inability to experience and understand these giant and mysterious creatures who live in an underwater world we can't fully penetrate, we might begin to think more like Cormac McCarthy, John Lilly, or Native peoples. As all of them suggest, perhaps whales do have access to all of the information that exists in the universe.

To reiterate their sentiments, the next time we find ourselves pondering existential questions, we may be wise to look to the whales for answers. And perhaps rather than think, what we really need to do is feel. The following stories offer unique examples of how people have used whales as guides—messengers capable of communicating wisdom without the use of words. These individuals' lives have been forever altered as a result of having listened.

DAVID NEIWERT: *What Killer Whales Can Teach Us*

The connection between David Neiwert and orcas isn't immediately apparent. The Seattle-based author is most known for his work as a contributing writer for the Southern Poverty Law Center's blog, *Hatewatch*, and for his books covering the radical right. He is not afraid to tackle tough subjects, although his favorite topic to talk about (and perhaps also write about) can be detected by taking a closer look at his blog, *Orcinus: Spyhopping the Right* (named after the unique way orcas sometimes spy at their above-water surroundings).

The book of his that he most enjoyed promoting, *Of Orcas and Men: What Killer Whales Can Teach Us,* also demonstrates his passion for cetaceans. He wrote the book when he desperately needed an emotional break from covering domestic terrorism, militias, and hate crimes. It was a book he'd always wanted to read, and he finally got tired of waiting for someone else to write it.

Of Orcas and Men beautifully integrates the unique characteristics of the biology, social lives, and intelligence of orcas with a digestible overview of the contemporary threats these apex predators face. Although David is primarily a scientific writer, elements of spirituality and wonder surface through the science. Even having achieved considerable success as an author, he remains—like the orca—social, relatable, and characterized by a great sense of humor.

David's career has come full circle back to his childhood dreams, in a way. Growing up in southeast Idaho, he became fascinated with dolphins after discovering the TV show *Flipper*. He chose the animal for multiple school reports and decided he wanted to become a marine biologist. However, after majoring in biology for his first two years at the University of Idaho, he determined, "I was not cut out for science at all." At least not in the practical sense.

What he really wanted to do was write about science. He changed his major to English and sought to become a journalist. "I still had a love for science and an ability to read scientific documents and explain them in layman's terms," he explained. And he was still interested in marine science. However, having lived only in landlocked Idaho and Montana, he had yet to see a whale or dolphin.

It was during his honeymoon that he first had the opportunity to see one—but unfortunately, his timing was off. David and his wife, Lisa, had moved to Seattle, and they took their trip to Alert Bay, off the northern tip of Vancouver Island, British Columbia. In the 1990s, whales were still quite plentiful there and commonly spotted in the summertime. And they were abundant the week before David and Lisa honeymooned, seen on whale watching trips every day—until the day they went whale watching.

The couple would spend the next two years chasing whales during visits to San Juan Island, Washington, but to no avail. "We'd show up off the west side of the island, and people there would say, 'Oh, you just missed them!' It was like they knew we were coming. My wife was convinced we were jinxed," David said.

Despite their poor luck, the couple kept pursuing their goal to see whales and dolphins in the wild. Aside from his personal interest, David knew that orcas were the consummate Northwest environmental story. Around them revolved everything from the area's iconic and endangered wild salmon population to pollution in the Salish Sea. "Everything else is wrapped up in this one animal," he realized, which is the theory he started with for a freelance writing assignment in 1995.

While conducting research for that article, David traveled to San Juan Island for an interview with Ken Balcomb of the Center for Whale Research. He and Lisa, who joined him as his "photo assistant," finally went out on a successful whale watching trip, along with Ken and a couple of other whale researchers. The crew encountered a pod of Transient orcas, and the experience was as awe-inspiring as David had imagined it would be.

More articles about orcas were in David's future. So were other topics. While he was writing about this quintessential Northwest animal, he started to write about the seemingly unrelated topic of the evolution of Northwest militias. He had a long-running relationship with the Southern Poverty Law Center from years as a premier reporter on hate crimes and extremism.

By the late 1990s, he was making regular trips out to San Juan Island, spending a week or two kayaking and camping. He did so not only because he was writing about whales but because he was being drained writing about human hatred. "Going out there was really an important part of maintaining my life balance," he explained. "It met the internal, emotional needs I required after writing so much on the topic of hate crimes. I'd developed a medical examiner's approach to the topic, but even so, it brings you down after a while, so hanging out with the whales became spiritual sustenance for me."

His visits to the island became more regular after his daughter was born in 2001, due to his desire to offer her the outdoor experiences that have been his source of spiritual strength. He started taking her camping on the west side of San Juan Island in 2002. She had her first wild orca encounter in 2003, while kayaking. He wrote about the experience in his book *Of Orcas and Men*. They were not expecting to see orcas that day, as sightings in the area had been sparse that week. However, after David's daughter, Fiona, began singing, the family was treated to a close encounter with a pod of orcas.

He's not entirely certain that the three-note melody from *The Little Mermaid* she sang was responsible for the incredible encounter; however, it did make him wonder. The whales were in rapid-transit mode and cruising in another direction when she began to sing—and that was precisely when they changed course and made a slow pass by their kayak. Close enough for David to get a fresh whiff of whale breath.

Not bad for a family who had previously been jinxed. "The deal with whales is you've got to get on whale time," David said. "We had to stop chasing them and just sort of be where they tend to be. Pretty soon the whales will come along."

He would have another powerful orca encounter in 2010, with the orca known as J28, or Polaris. The mother orca was nuzzling her newborn calf. The father of a young child himself, David understood how important physical contact is in establishing a close relationship between parent and child. "Watching those two together, I thought, 'Yeah, I know what's going on there.' Witnessing that," he said, "you realize how close to human they are. They love—not just like us, but maybe even more deeply than we do. That was really profound to me."

Prior to those experiences, he had sought to give his daughter encounters with orcas by going to SeaWorld, something he later regretted. "I hadn't really worked through the whole captivity thing yet. It wasn't until after we'd gone to the show a couple of times when I realized it just didn't feel right. After you see them in the wild, you can't help but feel that way. In the wild, they swim constantly for up to one hundred miles a day. Putting an animal like that in a tiny little pool is torturous."

His feeling against captivity was accentuated when he learned about how orcas use echolocation, the detection of objects using the reflection of sound. "They experience horrible sensory deprivation in those tanks. It's like putting a human in a white room and locking the door," David said and quoted Lori Marino, a neuroscientist and expert in animal behavior and intelligence: "Orcas are the most acoustically sophisticated animals on the planet."

He added, "They communicate on an acoustic level we can't even begin to comprehend. There's so much going on within those calls. They can even see inside of each other." The latter is the fascinating result of their ability to transmit images using sound. They can detect illness, for example, in each other and in humans. If that's not enough of a sign of intelligence, consider the physicality of orca brains.

Compared to the human brain, the orca brain has been functioning in a sophisticated fashion for several million years, whereas the modern human brain has existed for only two hundred thousand years. Research by Lori Marino reveals that the orca brain has a whole part that the human brain does not: a lobe of tissue in the paralimbic region that performs unknown functions. What is known is that the lobe (which is highly elaborated in most cetaceans, not just orcas) has something to do with processing emotions and thinking. This leads a curious human to at least wonder what whales might know that we don't.

"It's pretty hard not to conclude that they're incredibly intelligent," David shared. "But how do you define that intelligence? In their world, we're really stupid orcas, and in our world, they're really stupid humans." He paused before adding with a smile, "But even then, they're probably smarter humans than we are orcas."

Kidding aside, "it's amazing how much like us they are, or how much like them we are." We both exhibit apex predator behaviors, social aspects, and the desire to dominate the ecosystem. In social situations, however, orcas don't display aggression the way we can. Squabbles between Transient orcas and Resident orcas happen, although rarely. "In general, they demonstrate an incredible amount of cooperativeness," David said. "They are also a matriarchal society, which I think has tremendous advantages. If we try to follow that path, I believe that will help us."

There's a lot we can learn from observing orcas, David feels. "Just look at their social structures and you'll realize we have a lot to learn. The lines between the individual and the group are really blurred; they're connected socially at a really deep level.

"These animals have been apex predators of the ocean for 6 million years. Humans are trying to displace them as the top species on the planet, and we kind of have, but I don't know how long we're going to stay there. Certainly, what we're doing now is not sustainable. We don't seem to have the longevity thing figured out."

David suggested that we'd be wise to look at orcas and start asking questions: What have been the keys to their longevity? What can orcas teach us about ourselves and our relationship with the natural world? How can we evolve in a way that actually makes us a more productive species that's better for the planet?

David explained that, for one thing, orcas seem to voluntarily limit and moderate their populations. They also seem to limit their consumption; they don't eat everything in their path, even though they could. They're not wasteful like humans; they don't kill for the sake of killing. On an emotional level, they are empathetic. "I think that has a lot to do with their ability to survive," he explained. "As humans, we are losing our ability to empathize. Especially with the internet, people aren't relating to each other in normal human ways anymore."

We could also take cues from the orcas by underlining our actions with a sense of humor and playfulness. "Orcas like to play games and mess with your head. They have an exquisite sensitivity to feelings and thoughts that can be truly mind-boggling." He shared stories of how, back when every camera used film, the orcas seemed to sense that there were a finite number of frames on a single roll. When David was out on Ken Balcomb's research boat, Ken insisted that they displayed the most interesting behavior only after a roll of film ran out.

David shared that Ken has also had experiences where the whales seem to understand and do exactly what he wanted. With the birth of a new calf, the researcher needs to see the underbelly of the whale to determine its gender. "They've gotten to know Ken so well that the mothers come over to him and have their baby turn over."

He shared another time when orcas seemed to read his mind. "I was in Johnstone Strait, observing a mother and calf and a large male from my kayak. I had heard that Northern Resident killer whales aren't as demonstrative as the Southern Residents, and that is what I observed—they were all business. Just as I put my camera down and thought to myself, 'It's true—they're nondemonstrative,' the big male breached fifteen feet in front of me." David sat in awe of the acrobatic, above-water leap the whale performed.

Having once studied to be a scientist, David is aware of the human tendency to anthropomorphize, or project human traits onto animals. However, certain situations "you really can't explain any other way," he said. He has attempted to figure out the phenomenon. "Perhaps it's because we actually speak our thoughts inaudibly. When we're thinking a thought, they may be able to pick up on it because it's actually coming out of our vocal chords in a way we can't hear but they can."

David's ability to practice such exploratory thinking in a way that many scientists cannot is what makes David's career as a writer that much more rewarding. *Of Orcas and Men* may not have been written had he not had an insatiable desire to read a book that put all the pieces together—one that was not just about orcas, their biology, or their captivity but about their role in the entire food chain and ecosystem.

Aside from the need for a comprehensive collection of killer whale themes, David understood that what is known about killer whales today is far more extensive than what was known at the time many of those other books on orcas were written. "It's phenomenal how much we've learned and yet we're still scratching the surface. Orcas are the best science subjects, because the more you know the more you realize how little you know."

Even though he knew there was a need for the book he had in mind, David always felt too busy to write it himself. Then came a moment when he desperately needed to. "In 2013, I published a book about vigilantes. I covered the case of a woman who was on death row. It was a horrible case, dealing with the dark side of the American psyche. By the time I finished writing it, I was a hollow shell." It was time for him to write "that orca book," he decided.

By doing so, he got to explore creative writing aspects he wasn't able to with the other styles of writing he'd done. "Hate crime is such a serious subject that you have to write in a serious tone. You can't be humorous. There's a lot of absurdity in that world, and I don't mind teasing that out, but I've always felt constrained. I have a nice, dry sense of humor, and I enjoy laughing, and I was never able to put that in my work." But he could with the orca book. "It was a lot of fun to write. I felt like I was reaching young people, but older people too. The idea was to write something that would hit that sweet spot."

Although David attests there are many methods of communication that can be used to educate and inspire others, the role of a writer is unique. "I see the writer's job as one that explains or explores the world with other people. The only medium of exchange we have that works in our minds is the literal. It's words that we rearrange logically to approach the world rationally."

He knew he'd managed to communicate his ideas in a clear and compelling way, but still he had difficulty marketing the book to publishers. His persistence paid off when the manuscript was finally accepted by Overlook Press (which got its name because it features authors who have been overlooked by larger publishers). "They did a great job with it. They designed a lovely cover and pretty much just let me write the book I wanted," he said.

He had a lot of fun promoting and selling the book too. "I got to talk about orcas for a change instead of these dark subjects," he shared. He would introduce his talks by saying to the audience, "Orcas are the coolest animals on the planet, and I'm going to tell you why."

Audience and reader response was enthusiastic—to the point where one woman even told him she became a marine naturalist and began working at the Whale Museum on San Juan Island as a result of having read his book. "That made me feel good. I haven't even been able to get my daughter to read it," David quipped. "She's a teenager, and I'm, like, really stupid now."

Whether she's read her father's book or not, his daughter serves as the inspiration for David to continue sharing what he has learned about the orcas and to take personal action for their protection. "She's ultimately my motivation for all of this—it's not to make things better for me, it's for these next generations. I don't want to leave the world a worse place than it was when I came in."

In fact, he believes that the ability for our species to have future generations hinges on our ability to usher other species back from the brink of extinction. In the case of the Southern Resident killer whales of the Pacific Northwest, there isn't much time left.

"I'm working on an article now about how dire their situation is," David shared. "The local newspaper runs all kinds of stories and headlines when there are killer whale births. They love to run the feel-good stories but not to tell you about what's really going on. People in the Seattle area don't know they're down to seventy-six whales, and they're starving."

He continued, "People are painting murals of orcas on buildings without realizing we're about to lose them. We have this national treasure here, and to let it just slip through our fingers because of negligence is infuriating. It makes me want to fight."

Although the overall picture of the sustainability of the Southern Resident killer whale species looks bleak, there is a core group of deeply committed people acting on their behalf. Unfortunately, in the bureaucratic system we live with today, what David believes is needed more than anything is political action—and not too many orca activists are politically savvy.

In an effort to boost media coverage and hopefully attract attention from government figures, David organized a major press conference on the Seattle waterfront in October 2016, after the death of the orca J28 (Polaris), whom he'd witnessed six years earlier nuzzling with her calf. The mother is presumed to have died from birthing complications, and despite the efforts of other female pod members to feed J28's latest calf, J54 (Dipper), the latter soon died of malnutrition.

In January 2018, the Center for Whale Research, the nonprofit organization DamSense, and twenty-two thousand petitioners and supporters took out a full-page ad in the *Seattle Times* to inform state officials of the crisis surrounding the endangered Southern Resident killer whales and ask for their support in breaching the four Lower Snake River dams that impede the passage of salmon, the main food source for the starving orca population.

"Our politicians are not recognizing how critical the situation is and are utterly failing to take action," David stated. If the people with the decision-making power aren't paying attention, what can we do? He suggested that aside from obtaining media coverage and writing and calling our representatives, we ultimately need to take personal responsibility for the situation the orcas and the ecosystem are in through our daily practices.

David offered one situation we do have control over: "If I use chemicals on my lawn here in Seattle, it will kill the salmon runs out there in the sound and make fewer salmon available for the killer whales. If we're going to save the megafauna, we have to save the whole system. Orcas can be an icon for inspiring action. It's not just these whales that need saving—it's their whole world that needs saving. It's a big task, but there's a thousand things we can all do to make a difference in our daily lives and also by engaging on a higher level politically."

Cultivating a more holistic mindset plays a significant role in the future of all species. He shared, "I mentioned in my book that in Norway there was once a competition to kill the last salmon; the mindset at the time was all about conquering everything. That ethos has pretty much gone away. We're realizing how destructive it is, so I think we have a chance at turning things around." For David, saving the orcas is an indicator of whether or not we can save ourselves. "If we are able to keep this population viable even in the face of all these challenges, it means maybe we're not so hopeless after all."

Although David initially explained how writing a book about orcas helped him to recover emotionally and spiritually after a career focused on hate crimes, it later became apparent that a deeper connection between hate crimes and orcas existed beneath the surface. "I came to the realization that the negation of hate groups—of evil and human destruction—is empathy, love, community and humanitarian values. Those qualities play a big part in what I think killer whales have to teach us. Empathy and love for each other."

For more information on David Neiwert's books and blog, visit www.dneiwert.blogspot.com. Photo by Lisa Dowling.

CARRIE NEWELL: *Gray Whale Encounters*

Carrie Newell's magnetic presence can be felt whenever and wherever she speaks about whales—whether it be while teaching marine biology at Lane Community College in Eugene, Oregon; guiding whale watching tours out of Depoe Bay, Oregon; or leading ecotourism trips to the gray whale birthing lagoons off the Baja California Peninsula in Mexico.

Had someone not already developed a passion for marine mammals before meeting her, they would be highly likely to within minutes of listening to Carrie speak. Her animated instruction and enthusiasm for marine life—particularly gray whales—is contagious. She ignites a passion for the subject in whomever has the great fortune to be in a classroom with her or on one of her whale watching boats.

The most-asked question at the Whale, Sea Life and Shark Museum in Depoe Bay by visitors wanting to go on a whale watching trip is "Can I be on Carrie's boat?" Once you meet her—or even see a video of her, such as in Jean-Michel Cousteau's *The Gray Whale Obstacle Course*—you'll understand why people come from all over the world to be out on the ocean with her.

Contrary to what one might suspect, Carrie did not grow up near the ocean. She never even saw a whale in the wild until she was in her mid-twenties. She is originally from Michigan, so she did enjoy major bodies of water—the Great Lakes. "I would swim in Lake Huron and pretend I was a dolphin or a researcher working with Jacques Cousteau. I would envision what it might be like to be a marine biologist."

It was through watching episodes of *The Undersea World of Jacques Cousteau* and *Flipper* that her passion for marine biology developed, but Carrie believes she was born with an interest in biology in her blood. One of her earliest memories is spending time on her grandparents' farm, wading through the nearby river and the mud, collecting tadpoles and frogs and fish.

A trip to Florida at the age of thirteen sealed her love for the ocean, even though she did not encounter any major marine life. "That was the only trip my family ever went on as I grew up," she began. "I had saved up fifty dollars and I spent all of it at Sea Shell City on specimens, which I still have in my museum to this day!"

Though her vision for the future was always pointed in the direction of the ocean, it took a while for her to get there. She married at the age of twenty and moved with her husband to South Dakota. She took one year of college classes at South Dakota State University (SDSU) before moving with her husband to Utah. She continued studying in Utah, transferring credits back to SDSU, and completed a wildlife and fisheries degree, followed by another bachelor's degree in biology and geology.

Carrie was nine months pregnant with her older daughter, Amber, when her life direction was guided by her husband's job again—this time to Arizona. After their daughter was born, Carrie began teaching a bird class at Yavapai College near Cottonwood, Arizona, though she considered herself a mediocre birder at best. Five and a half years later, her second daughter, Ariel, was born. (Ariel later became the first deckhand on her mother's boat!)

During her early years of teaching, Carrie was not the informed teacher she would yet become. "When I first started to teach, I just read the book and reiterated what I read," she said. "Now I teach everything from experience, but I didn't have enough experience at that point in my life." To prepare for her bird classes, she went to every field trip site in advance and used her bird book to identify those she saw.

Meanwhile, she pursued further academic study of her own and earned a master's degree in biological science/aquatic zoology from Northern Arizona University. Not long after that, she would finally see her first whale. She was in Puerto Peñasco, Mexico, when she saw a fin whale—just briefly, way off shore. Perhaps it was a glimpse of what was to come; she and her husband split up soon after, which opened up an opportunity for her to fully pursue her own path. It was one that would be guided by whales.

Carrie shared that she has been described as a visionary, and while she may underestimate the length of time it takes to reach her goals, she perseveres, and she eventually gets where she wants to go. "In 1992, I took both my girls and a dog and moved to Eugene, Oregon," Carrie said. She had been offered a full-time position teaching biology at Lane Community College. "I had no home, no friends, no nothing. I just had a job." She's been there ever since—there, and Depoe Bay, Oregon. She saw her first gray whale ever from Cape Foulweather near Depoe Bay, which influenced her decision to work in the area.

Depoe Bay is the self-proclaimed whale watching capital of the Oregon Coast, and therefore an area Carrie naturally gravitated toward. While working as a biology professor, she became interested in doing research in relation to the population of gray whales that didn't complete the typical migration route from Baja California to the Arctic but stopped instead at Depoe Bay to stay from June through October.

In the late 1990s, after having observed the whales spending a significant amount of time hanging out in kelp beds, she decided to study the reason behind their behavior. Research published at the time indicated that gray whales ate amphipods, which Carrie knew (from having earned a master's degree on the topic) lived primarily in mud, not rocks, where kelp beds grow. Depoe Bay had a muddy bottom, so she suspected the whales were dining on the abundance of mysid shrimp among the kelp, and was able to prove that by studying the whales' fecal matter.

Not only was that discovery what got her foot in the door to the PhD program at Oregon State University but it led to her being contacted by Cousteau's Ocean Futures Society. Carrie was invited to work with the Cousteau film and dive crew—alongside Jacques Cousteau's son, Jean-Michel—in the summer of 2004. Her childhood dream had come true.

Carrie's career, and the pursuance of her passion, began to take off. She completed her fourth degree in biological oceanography, earned her captain's license, and bought her first boat, a twenty-two-foot Zodiac. She combined her two passions, teaching and whale watching, to form her own company, Whale Research EcoExcursions. She currently owns four boats, twenty-two-to-thirty-six-foot Zodiacs, which she and her team use to take visitors out on tours in pursuit of primarily gray whales. She also leads an annual trip to the gray whale breeding lagoons in Mexico.

Carrie has opened a museum in Depoe Bay, which houses everything from her childhood shell collection to over twenty sets of shark jaws, hundreds of marine life specimens, and several books she has written and published herself—including a guide to identifying the more than seventy gray whales that consistently make the Oregon Coast their summer home. She also sells framed prints of remarkable photographs she has taken of marine life throughout her many years out on the ocean.

To say she keeps busy is an understatement; she commutes from her home in Eugene (where she teaches during the week) to her home in Depoe Bay (where she leads whale watching trips on weekends and during the summer months). It is not uncommon for her to spend eight, ten, or even twelve hours a day out on a boat.

And she's not even a coffee drinker. She shared that it gives her a "high" to teach. "I love people, I love teaching, and I love nature, so even though the days can be long, my job is fulfilling. When I can show someone the gray whale mothers and their calves, or the orcas or baby seals or whatever it may be, it's an adrenaline rush for me. And I think that's what keeps me going."

Even after all of these years, since she never knows what she's going to see, she never gets bored being out on the water. She never gets tired of experiencing other people's reactions to the whales, either. She delights in offering visitors unforgettable experiences. "I love taking people out who have never seen a whale. They get so excited!"

As does Carrie. Her face lit up as she began to share a story. "Last summer I had a lady on the boat from France, and I was telling her about Comet. Comet is the name I've given to a whale I can call up to the boat. The lady didn't believe I could do it, but we went out there, and I saw Comet, and I called her right up to the boat. The lady cried her eyes out."

That was not an isolated incident. "Whales like Comet and Eagle Eye and Scarback that I've seen for many years, some since 1992, I think they recognize my boat and my voice." Just like Carrie's students and passengers, the whales likely feed off of her enthusiasm and are potentially even physically drawn to it. Of course, the whales don't know it, but her boats are even named after some of them—including Comet and Eagle Eye.

"It's a highlight of my life, being able to share that passion with others," Carrie continued. "For example, today I had a family from India on the boat, and we had orcas going underneath the boat on their side and looking at us. And the lady kept putting her hands together and bowing her head: 'Thank you, thank you.' Being able to give people these amazing life experiences is just wonderful."

Carrie isn't only a witness to other people's experiences—she has intimate experiences of her own. "There have been times when those whales have looked me right in the eye, as if we're truly connecting." And not just with Carrie but with her golden retriever, Kida. Many people knew Kida as Carrie's "first mate." For the nearly sixteen years of her life, Kida would go out on the boat with Carrie and get just as excited about whale encounters as the captain.

"She was so good at finding whales," Carrie recalled. "Her right ear would go up if the whale was on the right, and her left ear would go up if the whale was on the left. Even in the fog, all of the other boats would go by, but Kida would bark, so I knew there was a whale around. She was my secret weapon."

Kida took a particular interest in one whale, Blanco—and vice versa. "Kida would hang over the side and Blanco would come over and blow in her face. He liked to tease my dog. One day Kida jumped in the water and ended up right next to Blanco's head. I immediately pulled her out—it freaked me out—but Blanco and Kida thought it was great." Carrie has pictures of that encounter—along with additional shots of Blanco looking right into Kida's eyes.

Carrie has spent so much time with many of the individual whales that she has come to recognize their unique personalities.

Blanco, for example, likes to chase females but often gets ditched, so he then seeks out interaction with people (or Carrie's dog). Eagle Eye is known as a romantic. "He comes here, and he chases females." Carrie smiled. "A couple of years ago, he showed up mid-July and courted females all summer; they were females that couldn't get pregnant, but he sure liked practicing a lot."

Carrie got quiet and thoughtful as she reflected on the more powerful experiences she's had with the whales—ones that, even for a scientist, hint at something otherworldly. "Kida was diagnosed with cancer in 2016. Her health had started to go down, but I took her out on the boat, and I saw Scarback. Scarback came right up to the boat, the same side Kida was on, and fluked." Each lobe of a whale's tail is known as a fluke; when the tail is displayed above water, the whale is said to have "fluked"—which is a stunning and somewhat rare occurrence to catch up close. "She kept coming up to the boat and fluking repeatedly. We stayed with her for quite a long time, and then we went farther south and saw some other whales. And just when I told the people on the boat that we needed to return to the dock, Scarback came back again, right next to the boat."

It's an emotional memory for Carrie to recall. "That was the last encounter Kida had on the ocean, because she got really bad. But in my mind, that was God saying, 'Here is your favorite whale and your favorite dog. I'm going to give you a really good encounter.' Kida looked right into my eyes on that trip, and I knew that would be the last trip with her." She passed shortly thereafter.

Another experience when Carrie felt what she called God occurred right after her dad died. "I went out on the ocean, and I saw Comet from a distance. I said, 'God, if Dad's in heaven, can you have Comet come up here and just fluke in that sea foam right by the boat?' The next thing I knew, Comet fluked right next to us in the sea foam. And then in my mind, I thought, 'You know, I'd really like to see her breach.' Within seconds, she breached, and I got it on video. Then I thought, 'That was really cool, but I'd really like a still shot of that. Could you have her breach again?' She breached again, and I got a beautiful still shot of her." Breaching gray whales are not a common occurrence, making the incident incredibly special.

As if she needed to be further convinced of a spiritual side of life and a capacity for whales to communicate seemingly telepathically, Carrie experienced another amazing connection. She lost her mechanic, Tom, during an accident while he was working on her boat. The incident devastated her, but she soon received a reassuring message. "The week before he died, we went out on the ocean together, and a whale named Lucky breached right next to us. When I finally brought my boat back in the water after his death, who shows up again but Lucky, breaching alongside us."

That wasn't all. "I had given his widow yellow roses a couple of days before, and she told me that's what they'd had at their wedding. Now, I was far out on the ocean—there was no other boat—and all of a sudden, I had this overwhelming smell of roses. I asked the other people on my boat if they smelled something, and they said, 'Yeah, I smell roses!'"

Carrie looked incredulous, recalling the event. "There were just too many weird things, too many times. What I believe is that God was saying, in all those instances, that Dad's in heaven, Tom's in heaven, and Kida will meet you in heaven too. Because I don't know what else it could be."

Amid other tragic situations occurring on the planet, Carrie has most likely had to reach for that same faith in order to remain optimistic. One of her biggest concerns is for the Southern Resident orcas, whose population is steadily decreasing due to dam impediment, among other factors, causing low salmon supply—the staple of their diet. "That and the Great Pacific Garbage Patch are worrisome to me. I always tell my students to try not to drink bottled water. I usually have my aluminum container with me. And don't use plastic bags because they end up in the Garbage Patch."

She practices what she preaches in other ways too. "I don't put pesticides or herbicides on anything on my property. I have half an acre with lots of fruit trees. Sometimes I have worms in my apples, but oh well, it's extra protein." She laughed. "GMOs are another pet peeve of mine. What we put in our foods and into our bodies will go into our water supply and eventually into the oceans."

As an educator, however—especially one with a natural ability to inspire others—Carrie has reason to be hopeful. Jacques Cousteau is known for having said that people protect what they love. "If you instill a love for the whales in people, guess what? They'll want to save those whales. Or whatever it is—any animal or aspect of nature. The Audubon Society saved the Great Egret from extinction after being heavily hunted in the late 1800s for its plumes. So, the various societies out there working toward conservation give me hope too."

Although Carrie does what she can to pass her passion for whales and the oceans on to her students and whale watching passengers, she understands that education must begin at home. She raised her two daughters to be nature lovers and stewards and is an advocate for pursuing self-education both in and out of the classroom.

To youth and adults who have a passion for marine biology but don't live near an ocean, Carrie recommends reading every book they can on the subject. "Adopt a whale, watch videos, and look for anything you can do related to biology. Try to volunteer somewhere even if it's not with whales—just get connected with nature. And if marine biology is something you know you want to do, hold that vision and make sure you don't stray from that path. It won't be easy. You're going to have to work long and hard to get to where you want to get, but don't give up."

She continued, "Think about what your ultimate purpose is in this life and go for it. I believe all of us have special talents and skills that will enhance our purpose if we keep open-minded enough to figure out what that purpose is. It may not be what you do for a job; maybe it's something you do in your spare time."

It's safe to say Carrie has found her purpose. It's read on the faces of everyone she teaches or takes out on the water. She shared, "I've had people come up to me after trips and say, 'This has been the best day of my whole life.' And if you can give someone what they consider the best day of their *whole* life...I mean, what else can you ask for?"

Visit www.oregonwhales.com *for more information on Carrie's whale watching tours, the Whale, Sea Life and Shark Museum, and the various books she has published on marine life in the Pacific Northwest.*

ANNE GORDON DE BARRIGON: *Whale and Dolphin Wisdom*

Anne Gordon de Barrigon's childhood and career were enriched by many opportunities to engage with wild animals. She grew up with killer whales and other marine mammals practically in her backyard, and she can count working in a zoo, maintaining her own array of exotic animals, and training animals for the film industry among her many experiences.

No species, however, has intrigued her quite as much as whales and dolphins. For a while, she couldn't quite put into words what made them distinct. After embarking on her own spiritual journey, she was able to piece together the puzzle: they embodied the spiritual beliefs she had begun to claim as her own. They lived in overall harmony, transparency, and community. They possessed a deep-seated wisdom that she began to tap into as transferable to the human race.

Some humans already have established tribes similar to whale and dolphin pods—one of these is the Emberá tribe, located in a remote village in Panama. After being hired to work with the tribe for a film shoot, Anne fell in love with not only the way of life that defined the community but a particular member of the tribe. The union led her to leave her animal training business, move to Panama, and open the first whale watching company in the country. Additionally, she hosts Whale and Dolphin Wisdom Retreats, at which she shares the lessons she has learned from the species she has come to refer to as her "soul family."

She may be an honorary member of an indigenous Panamanian tribe, but Anne's roots are in the Pacific Northwest. During the first eleven years of Anne's life, her family made several trips to the Oregon Coast from their hometown of Eugene, Oregon. Then, after the family moved to Olympia, Washington—on the southern tip of Puget Sound—the sea became part of Anne's daily existence. She recalled doing her high school homework while seated on the beach, watching killer whales pass by.

Even then, she knew she was witnessing something majestic. "Whenever I saw orcas, they always exuded a very comforting presence, almost like having a protective big brother around. It's impossible for most people not to smile when they see an orca or a dolphin. Even though they were always around, I could never get enough of them!"

Her intrigue increased exponentially when she took a marine biology course in high school; overnight camping trips to the Olympic Peninsula and her teacher's infectious enthusiasm instilled in her a passion for the topic and the recognition that she, too, could pursue a career doing what she loved. She went on to earn a biology degree from Western Washington University with a minor in psychology, "which was really every animal behavior course they had," and secured a job at Seattle's Woodland Park Zoo. She became the first woman hired to work as a keeper in the zoo's carnivore unit.

Anne didn't much like routine, however, which is something zoo animals depend on. Plus, she wanted more interaction with the animals than the zoo was able to offer. After three years, the time had come for a change. Her next steps were facilitated by a task her employer assigned to her. The zoo had a pair of lion cubs whose mother died during childbirth; since they couldn't be reintroduced into the pride, they were sold to a company in Southern California that taught people how to train wild animals. Anne was asked to deliver them.

When she arrived, she was drawn into the possibility of being able to have more hands-on interaction with wild animals. She asked for a job but settled for a temporary volunteer position. After eight months in the position, she had gained an incredible amount of experience and education training lion and tiger cubs, camels, zebras, chimpanzees, leopard cats, and more—but her savings was running out. She accepted a raccoon she had raised and trained as "severance pay," which she used to begin her own animal education outreach business back in Washington.

Before long, she could have opened her own zoo. "I had a raccoon, wolf pup, reindeer, tiger, and lion. It was really fun!" Anne smiled. "It wasn't a huge moneymaker, but I was able to go out a couple times per week and speak to auditoriums of children." After five years managing that business, she felt called to launch another business venture. She realized no one was providing animals for movies and TV in the Pacific Northwest. She learned how to apply the training she had to film work. She rehomed the wild animals in her care—which again freed her from demanding daily routines— and for the next eighteen years focused on freelance film work. She trained animals used in movies such as *Legends of the Fall*, *Homeward Bound*, and *Practical Magic*.

Anne loved her job and was successful at it, but something was missing. She felt she'd disengaged from her spirit. Her earlier love of whales and dolphins had been brushed aside in pursuance of what appeared to be more lucrative. She began studying meditation and reading books about spirituality. "Then I started feeling a real strong call from the dolphins," she said. "I booked a whale watching trip on Orcas Island [Washington] for my birthday, and that ended up being one of those magical days when there was a superpod." All three Southern Resident orca populations were present and performing an array of incredible antics. The experience brought back Anne's childhood memories of being with the orcas.

She was living in California and started spending every weekend walking the beach. Without fail, she'd see dolphins and sometimes gray whales breaching. She even swam with the dolphins once— she couldn't see them, but she could hear them communicating underwater. At the same time, she discovered Mary Getten's book *Communicating with Orcas*, which opened her mind to the possibility of interspecies communication.

Not long after she dove headfirst into her studies of whale and dolphin wisdom, she was hired to work on a film shoot in Panama. Indigenous people were hired as actors. After she had spent only a few days with them in their village located deep within the rainforest, her fascination with the culture grew. She instinctively recognized the similarities between the tribe and cetacean pods (such as dolphins and orcas). The tribe lived in unity, community, and transparency. "They have very few clothes, their houses have no walls, everybody knows everything about everyone—and it works!" Anne said. "They are joyful and playful and so quick to laugh. Family is honored first, and uniqueness and independence are respected—exactly like a dolphin pod."

Anne fell in love with the tribe and with a man, who would soon become her husband. She left California and her freelance business and moved with her husband to a home outside the Panamanian village. The village's main source of income was tourism, and Anne saw a work opportunity. She was a native English speaker and had an insider's perspective of the tribe. She started her own tour guide business. Within a week, she had booked her first tour.

Meanwhile, the seeds for another business were sprouting in her mind. "I also kept thinking about how I was in a country with two oceans only fifty miles apart. Where were the whales and dolphins? What species were in the area, and how could I get out there to see them?" It took Anne two years of research to discover the answers to those questions.

"I learned that Panama, along with Costa Rica, are the only places in the world where humpbacks come from both hemispheres to breed and give birth. The migration route for the ones from the southern hemisphere is one of the longest known to man because it crosses the equator." She shared that from July to October the "southerners" are everywhere; there are over two thousand on the Pacific coastline and about nine hundred in the Pearl Islands. Then from December to March, approximately three hundred humpbacks arrive from North America.

"We get fewer northerners because this is the southern tip of their migration, and they stop anywhere from Mexico to here. For the southerners, Panama is their main destination because it's so protected here; there are warm, shallow waters and no predators in the inner areas—which is exactly what they're looking for."

Anne learned these basic facts but had yet to see humpbacks in Panama. In 2007, she hired a local fisherman to help offer her that first experience. They cruised out to the Pearl Islands and ended up encountering a pod of forty spotted dolphins and four humpback whales (and that was supposedly the slow season for whale watching). "I got in the water and swam with the dolphins and the whales," she remembered. "It was amazing. Such an incredible experience."

Since she was already operating village tours, she figured, why not add whale watching tours to her repertoire? Hers was the very first company in Panama to offer the service. "It was a bit of an uphill battle because nobody knew we had whales," Anne said. "When I first started the business, I'd tell Panamanians we were going whale watching, and they'd say, 'We have whales? Aren't they dangerous fish?' So, it's been a major process to educate the locals as well as the tourists."

Starting from scratch incited unique challenges. "I was doing everything on a shoestring budget. I didn't have money to launch advertising campaigns or to go to travel fairs around the world in order to put Panama on the world whale watching map. I did what I could, though. There are a couple of tourism newspapers in town, and I took out little ads, and they did stories on our company."

She also joined the World Cetacean Alliance, which hosted an annual festival called Whale Fest in the United Kingdom. "It was the largest whale festival in the world. I went there for three years and had a booth promoting whale watching in Panama. Through that alliance and their conventions, I met people from conservation protection groups, as well as people from whale and dolphin watching companies from around the world."

As a result of those connections, she was invited to participate as an expert advisor in the International Whaling Commission's (IWC) whale watching workshop in Brisbane, Australia; they wanted feedback on how to promote whale watching as opposed to whaling as an industry.

She was also invited to have a booth at an IWC meeting in Panama. She recalled the inner conflict she felt while surrounded by the Japanese delegation at the refreshment table. Japan's insistence on maintaining their controversial "scientific" or "subsistence" whaling practices (which result in the slaughter of thousands of dolphins and pilot whales per year from the town of Taiji) limited Anne to "talking about the cookies." Once in a more businesslike setting at the meeting, Anne tried to meet the Japanese IWC members on a human level. "Every single person is just trying to do the best they can for themselves and their family," she said. Their whaling practice is one she doesn't agree with, but she also recognizes the role it plays in Japanese culture.

"I've been to Japan four times, and I know how prideful they are." Anne believes that protesting has prolonged the dolphin hunting. The country is aware that there's no longer any nutritional need for the dolphin meat; Japanese scientist Tetsuya Endo found mercury levels (the second-most-toxic poison in the world) in dolphin and small-whale meat to be twenty to five thousand times higher than levels recommended by the UN World Health Organization and the Japanese Ministry of Health. Therefore, Anne believes, "The tradition would have probably died out by now if it weren't for the Japanese need to save face. Change will come not from telling them what to do—it has to come from within; the Japanese need to make that decision for themselves. The person who can stop the practice is someone who can make friends with and educate the mayor of Taiji. Let him be the hero, not the bad guy."

Anne's insight is one gained through years of spiritual study and study of wild dolphins and whales. By observing how they live and extrapolating that information to how humans could live by those principles, she not only has improved her own relationships but has developed a unique angle for her business. "I get my passion and juices flowing when I get to bring in that spiritual component to my tours and retreats."

She also has gained insights through observing humans watching whales. "It's impossible not to smile in the presence of a dolphin or whale. People get joyful suddenly; their arms open, and emotional barriers are let down. Sometimes we get silent; sometimes we shout. We're just in our raw state, without feeling the need to hide it."

Watching whales helps us reach another important state, she said. "When you're in the presence of a dolphin or whale, you are right there in that present moment. It is virtually impossible to think about the bills stacked on your desk at home or the problems you have at work. You can't think about tomorrow or yesterday— it's not possible."

A lesson Anne has learned from the whales and that she teaches in her retreats is the theory of abundance. "Baleen whales are the largest creatures on earth, and they eat the smallest creatures. All they have to do is open their mouth, and they will be fed." She recalled reading a news story about a man from the US who got lost in the Amazon jungle for two weeks. He finally figured out how to get out, but he was starving. After having spent time with the Emberá tribe, she thought, "How can you live in the rainforest for two weeks and not find food?" She realized the answer: "When it comes to abundance, humans have these limiting beliefs. We don't even try to search for food in the wild, but in nature, food is everywhere. Animals know this, but we humans struggle with this concept."

Her favorite topic of whale wisdom to teach is that of transparency. A dolphin or orca can use echolocation to see prey species and even inside of each other. They can detect pregnancies, tumors, and even emotional states, since physical reactions occur as a result of emotions. "There are no secrets in an orca community," Anne said. "We humans feel that we have to hide parts of ourselves; that if people really knew us, they wouldn't love us, which is not true at all. If we could live in transparency, we could live with the freedom that comes with not having anything to hide."

Whales are also masters at transforming negative energy into positive energy. "When a storm comes and there are really big waves, do they dive and hide? No, they get more playful!" Anne exclaimed. "The whales love to breach in the storms! They learned to surf through the challenges. They take the energy of the storm and instead of fighting and resisting it, they use that energy to propel them higher and farther than they could have gone before.

And they get joy out of it!" Anne likes to imagine what is possible for humans who have learned to do the same.

The gray whales have a lesson for us about forgiveness. Despite being known to whalers as "devilfish" because they were one of the few species that would fight back when harpooned, they were heavily targeted in the industry. It took only five winter hunts to empty the gray whale birthing lagoons in Baja, Mexico. During the 1850s, an estimated twenty thousand gray whales migrated past California. Twenty years later, only two thousand were counted. Now, in the very same lagoons where they were nearly hunted to extinction, those gray whales are the friendliest whales on earth. Laguna San Ignacio is once again home to nursing gray whale mothers and calves and serves as a model of sustainable ecotourism.

"They are the only species of wild dolphins or whales that come up and seek human touch," Anne shared. "They literally push their babies—their most prized and valued possessions of which every instinct is about protection—up to boats so humans can touch them. That is the ultimate lesson in forgiveness." She added that some of those whales are old enough to remember having been hunted; it wasn't until the 1970s that whaling in the Baja, Mexico, birthing lagoons stopped. "If these whales can forgive us, how can we not forgive ourselves?" she proposed.

Anne has been witness to countless transformative experiences while giving her whale watching tours and retreats. One particular highlight was with a woman who had won a tour through a charity auction. "She wasn't particularly spiritual or even that much interested in whales and dolphins, but she decided to participate in the tour anyway," Anne explained. "She shared with me before the trip that her adult son had died the year before, and she was still having a lot of guilt and sadness. She did not talk much on the trip, but on the very last day, she came up to me, hugged me, and with a smile ear to ear, she said, 'Thank you, Anne. I now have permission to be happy again.' It was so beautiful, and the result of simply being with the whales for five days."

The experience wasn't an anomaly. Anne witnesses metamorphoses during all of her retreats. "I see people experience relief from being plugged in all the time. I see them laughing and playing and I see a softening in their faces from the time they arrive to the time they leave. They reconnect with nature, but also with themselves and their own natural inner joy." Anne paused, thinking, before adding, "I also see them reconnect to spirit. They open their minds to a new way of living. People feel rejuvenated and relaxed; they feel passion again and sometimes rediscover their life's purpose. I don't have to do much of anything to initiate that shift—I just informally share stories on the boat. It's the whales who are doing all the life-changing work."

The latter may be true, but no doubt Anne plays a role in creating the space people need to feel safe and supported. She is a natural motivator who, by example, encourages people to never give up on their dreams and to always follow their passion. "I've been told many times not to do something because it was 'ridiculous' or 'crazy' or 'doesn't make sense.' But by following my heart, I have had the most amazing adventures and experiences. I've had really low lows, but the really high highs make everything worth it."

Her work with the dolphins and the whales have brought to light her own life's purpose. "If I could boil down my life's purpose to one word, it's *respect*. Respect needs to be instilled in all walks of life, and most importantly respect for the planet and nature." Her respect for the whales can be observed in many ways, including the distance she allows them on her tours. "You can't have twenty boats chasing around two whales," she related. "It should always be the whale's choice to be with you or not."

Similarly, she demonstrates respect for nature with her recycling practices, all the while maintaining a nonjudgmental mindset for those around her who have not adopted those practices for themselves. "Here in Panama the whole idea of not littering and recycling is in its infancy. Poverty is a big problem; taking care of the environment can sometimes be a luxury. It shouldn't be, because if you don't take care of the earth, it doesn't take care of you, but to get to that big-picture mindset, you have to be out of basic survival mode where you're struggling to feed your family." She suggested, "If we can improve conditions for the entire world and give everyone opportunities and education in a world built upon respect, then our planet will become more and more sustainable."

Once again, she turns to the whales in order to see their perspective. "I see how gracious and patient the whales and dolphins are with us," she shared. Intuitively, she knows we as humans also need to be patient with each other. It may be harder to change the mindsets and instill new values in older adults, but in the youth of today, she finds hope. "Education is being done. Young people are coming up with some brilliant ideas on how to keep the world healthy and clean."

Furthermore, she implements the wisdom of the whales by practicing unity. "I am a strong believer in the inherent good of people and the fact that nobody really wants to damage or harm the earth or the world. The damage happens when our fears or backgrounds or traumas and anger get in the way. We need to stop with the hate and the name calling and instead work on finding common ground."

An example of how to put such a concept into practice is to manage our own mindsets and emotions, which Anne sometimes facilitates through guided meditation. She told a story: "I led a meditation once for a group that wasn't particularly spiritual; I wasn't even going to do it, but then one of them asked. There was a teenage boy in the group who was very hyperactive, and I wasn't sure he'd be able to sit still long enough to do the meditation. However, he went so deep.

"We were doing an exercise on forgiveness, and I had them visualize a dolphin hunter from Taiji standing in front of us. Afterward, the boy said that when I first said that, he visualized punching him in the face. But then I guided the group to meet the man on a heart-and-soul level and to realize he's just trying to feed his family in the only way he knows how. I told them to picture his heart and how full it was with love for his family. By the end, the boy understood it was better to educate the man than to fight him. He pictured himself giving the man a hug."

Anne concluded, "That's what gives me hope. The more we are able be like dolphins and whales—the more we can spread love and forgiveness—the more the world will change for the better."

For more information on Anne's Whale and Dolphin Wisdom Retreats, visit www.whaleanddolphinwisdomretreats.com. Photo by Meera Aminova.

HOWARD GARRETT: *Orca Culture*

Like the Southern Resident orcas he has studied for nearly forty years, Howard Garrett emanates humility and generosity of spirit. There's no telling how many writers, filmmakers, and activists have approached him over the years, seeking his perspectives on everything from the retirement of Miami Seaquarium's captive whale Lolita (also known as Tokitae), to the current state of the endangered Southern Resident orca population.

Howard has been interviewed for the documentaries *Blackfish*, *Voiceless*, and *Fragile Waters* and has been featured in David Neiwert's *Of Orcas and Men*. He has authored his own series of books aimed at middle-school students, titled Orcas in Our Midst. Any level of fame he may have reached among the global whale-loving community, however, is overshadowed by his modesty and authenticity.

With all the interview practice Howard has had, words and stories naturally roll off his tongue. It's as though they have been waiting for their chance to infect the next listener or reader or viewer with the fascination for these majestic animals he has felt since he first encountered them.

Howard will never forget the first time he saw orcas in the wild. His brother, Ken Balcomb, of the Center for Whale Research on San Juan Island, Washington, had invited him for a visit in the summer of 1976. Under contract with the National Marine Fisheries Service, Ken had just begun his photo-identification research work to assess the population size of the Southern Resident killer whales. Howard didn't know much about whales at that time, but he knew a remarkable experience when he saw one.

Ken put him to work driving the boat, and on that day, he and Howard encountered members of L-pod, a family of Southern Resident killer whales, having great fun with a baby harbor porpoise. As primarily fish-eaters, the orcas did not appear to be playing with their food but rather gently lifting the porpoise up on their rostrums and giving it a ride in between them. Even Ken had never seen anything like it, and though Howard would return to his life in Colorado after the visit, the experience stayed with him.

Four years later, he would have the opportunity to return to San Juan Island on a longer-term basis. "Ken and I had lunch one day, and he said, 'Why don't you come up and volunteer? We need field assistants—no pay involved, but we can offer room and board.'" By "room and board," Howard understood that Ken meant a tent or a camper, but he was up for an adventure. He reflected, "That plopped me right down in the vortex of where the new knowledge about Southern Resident orcas and whales around the world was fermenting."

If Howard were an orca, he would most likely be a Transient— the variant of the species that covers more unpredictable, scattered grounds. He "migrated" back and forth from New Mexico to California during his childhood and young adult years before taking a sabbatical from his university studies to travel throughout Canada and Europe for five years. Upon returning to New Mexico, he bought some land in the mountains and attempted a homesteading lifestyle before moving to southern Texas and working in the oil fields, "of all things." It wasn't long, however, before he returned to New Mexico and then moved to Colorado Springs, where he finished his sociology degree at Colorado College.

Human sociology and marine biology may seem like disparate avenues of study, but after returning to San Juan Island to assist Ken with his orca research, Howard saw an instant connection. He had studied communications and cultural transmission among humans and noticed that orca societies were exhibiting the same characteristics. As the results of Ken's then-four-year study began trickling in, first on the list of incredible discoveries was that there was not one but two completely distinct types of orcas in and around Washington waters.

Canadian researcher Mike Bigg hypothesized that there were

two in the mid-1970s (based on the analysis of each whale's unique saddle patch and dorsal fin), but now it was confirmed. The populations that became known as Resident orcas and Transient orcas have different diets and different styles of communication and have not interbred for hundreds of thousands of years, "which is totally unheard of in wildlife biology," Howard shared. "There's no other species out there with what we call 'cultural traditions' that are so embedded and ingrained over thousands of generations that they completely guide and determine behavior." Other than humans, of course.

It wasn't just Bigg's and Balcomb's research that led to those results. The acoustics research of Canadian whale scientist John Ford came in around the same time, revealing what he called different "dialects" among the orca populations—and not just among Residents and Transients but among the pods within each species. This discovery caught Howard's attention. "The fact that they exhibit different vocal repertoires and different behaviors among the pods, meaning their language is intertwined with the behavior...that's sociology!"

His college studies had revolved around the concept of "symbolic interactionism," which Howard described as "the theory within sociology that language is the mediator of culture and behavior on a micro level. Perceptions and behaviors are continually reinforced and redefined, interpreted and gradually adapted, but they're all taking place in those immediate interactions using the words learned while growing up." The whales were, in other words, using the language they learned while growing up to express their culture.

It wasn't surprising for Howard to make these connections, but in his words, "This was 1981, '82, and nobody was going to go that far! Nobody had even said the word *culture*. So, I just did my reality checks. I kept on going back to the theory, going back to the fieldwork, and seeing what was in the current science, and everything kept checking out. I thought, 'This is incredible! They are living according to learned cultures that they are expressing 24/7 with each other.' No other animal even comes close to that."

In paralleling the whales for several hours every day, Howard gained a sense of what was "normal" for the whales, or what an average day was like. He also got a sense that their communications must be immediate because they would collectively change behavior on a dime.

For example: "I remember clearly one summer morning, in came J-pod, followed by K-pod, followed by L-pod. They were coming in from the Pacific; they turned a corner to come north up Haro Strait, separated by about a quarter mile, and then they stalled and milled about. Within a few minutes, L-pod grouped up and turned around and went back out to the Pacific, while J- and K-pods continued up north. To me, it was an obvious decision point.

"We can make a very safe assumption that their travel patterns are pretty much based on where the fish are, so I would assume that they came into Haro Strait, did a quick scan, and among the eighty or so whales, came to a quick conclusion that 'Sorry, there's not enough for all of us, guys.' My sense is that when they experience the luxury of an abundance of fish, they will stay together. They like to socialize, to tighten up and get into superpod antics. They jump out of the water and are very loud acoustically. They'll party when they can, but when they have to work, they go to work."

Though Howard has spent nearly four decades observing orcas, he still is in "utter awe" of their mastery of their world, in other words, their complete fearlessness. When he considers that the dolphin family has existed for millions of years and over that expansive time period has known no predators, he realizes that such freedom from fear has allowed them to focus their large brains instead on the development of intelligence.

They demonstrate that intelligence in the form of cohesion, for one. "Their loyalty to each other is absolute," Howard shared. "In fact, it's more absolute than survival. There are times when they'll sacrifice themselves for each other. They have figured out how to live as top predators without overconsuming. We don't know what may have gone on millions of years ago. There may have been episodes where communities of orcas got imperialistic and started forcing their neighbors out and eating everybody else's food and growing to thousands and thousands before they learned, 'This isn't working!' and backed off."

Howard's considerations go beyond the orca's ability to ration. He entertains the notion that they're able to practice a kind of conscious contraception, or ability to calibrate how many members of their population current resources can support. Otherwise, he argued, why wouldn't females have a baby every three or four years?

"I think they keep their population comfortably under the carrying capacity of their environment so that there won't be a die off." He added solemnly, "Which, of course, now we have so decimated their foraging base that there is." Howard was referring to the extreme decline in the Southern Resident orca's primary food source, salmon, which led to the species being placed on the endangered species list in 2005.

Howard is quick to mention that relationships among orcas are not all about peace and harmony—there is friction between the Residents and Transients, for example—but the general rule among them is coexistence. "Nobody's taking anyone else's food, nobody's getting into anybody else's way. They manage to have extreme cultural differences with virtually no hostility. That's a good way to live on the planet."

Once Howard makes such observations and discoveries, he can hardly wait to share them, and he's always been like that. He served as a naturalist on whale watching boats in the San Juan Islands in 1981 and 1982 and in Massachusetts in 1983. Twice a day, he'd narrate whale facts and anecdotes to one hundred or so guests, developing a keen storytelling ability in the process.

Howard based himself in Gloucester, Massachusetts, for ten years, after having served three months on a research boat studying humpback whales in the Caribbean. In 1993, however, "it was time to leave." He gave his brother a call and was invited to return to San Juan Island. A sign that his return may have been predestined appeared on the highway just after Howard loaded up his Toyota and drove out of Massachusetts.

He said, "I passed a shopping mall with a movie theater with a big marquee. They had a surprise debut of a movie that hadn't hit the screens yet." Those with sharp memories may already be guessing which movie it was: *Free Willy*. Howard had heard that the wild footage was filmed around the San Juan Islands, so he pulled into the cinema parking lot and went right into the theater.

"I saw whales that I hadn't seen in ten years, bigger than life! I saw my J-pod and K-pod friends. It was really exciting. Better than the rest of the movie." Howard laughed before clarifying, "But the movie was good too." When Howard arrived on San Juan Island a week or two later, he learned that Ken had been approached by the producers of *Free Willy* to find a better home for Keiko, the film's star orca.

The producers of the film lived on Orcas Island and knew Ken knew whales (he was a world-renowned expert on orcas). "Ken took the inquiry very seriously. He dedicated that whole summer to the project. He researched every shred of evidence and advice he could find on the best way to put a long-term captive whale back in the ocean." Howard handled phone calls and media while Ken immersed himself in the task at hand.

"A trip was arranged for him to go to Mexico and talk to the owners of the marine park and meet Keiko. Ken spent a day playing recordings of calls to Keiko and recording him back, getting to know him. He developed a proposal for putting Keiko back into the ocean near Iceland, where he came from, and hopefully reconnecting him with his family. The five owners of the park came back out and said, 'OK, you've got the job. We will not make any agreement with anybody else for six months while you decide exactly how you're going to do this, and then we will make a deal.'"

Unfortunately, SeaWorld sabotaged that agreement. Representatives from the theme park flew into Mexico, and within hours, the Alliance of Marine Mammal Parks (which is dominated by SeaWorld) put out a press release saying that they were going to "save Keiko." They contacted the owner of the marine park in Mexico and convinced them that Ken was a "phony biologist" and a "radical activist" and that it would be detrimental to their business to cooperate with him. They called off the deal, with no backup plan.

However, a writer for *Life* magazine got wind of Keiko's deplorable conditions in the Mexico marine park and the fact that the facility was discussing his potential release into the wild. An article was published in their November 1993 issue titled, "Won't Somebody Please Save This Whale?" Widespread media attention led to so many people contacting the magazine wanting to help Keiko that a second phone line had to be set up. More calls were received about "Willy" than had been received for any other story in the last decade.

It became obvious to Warner Brothers and the captive whale industry that something had to be done in response to the public outcry. Without Ken's recommendations—and with a significant financial contribution from Seattle billionaire Craig McCaw—plans were made and executed to relocate Keiko to a new and improved aquarium in Newport, Oregon. There, Keiko was rehabilitated before being moved to a sea pen (an established cove or a bay with an anchored net closing off the mouth) off Iceland for further training—presumably to reunite him with his family and lose his dependence on humans.

However, with limited experience of what it takes to release a captive whale into the wild, the SeaWorld trainers and others involved in Keiko's transition to open waters seemed to discourage his independence. They were afraid of losing track of him. Nonetheless, contrary to mainstream media reports, Keiko gradually learned to thrive in his new environment, building stamina and successfully foraging. However, no effort had been made by the trainers and team to understand the tight family ties that orca societies have, and it is believed that Keiko was not able to find members of his pod. He died off the coast of Norway in December of 2003, one year after his release.

"So, I got all wrapped up in that too!" Howard exclaimed. "And that also verified that these are such capable whales. They really can make that adaptation from decades in captivity to a life in the wild, so long as they have a transition period and most especially if they can relocate their families."

Throughout the years that efforts were being made to rehabilitate and release Keiko, a new flame sparked in Howard's heart. In 1995, he began campaigning for the release of Lolita, whom Howard affectionately prefers to call Toki (short for Tokitae), from the Miami Seaquarium. Since Ken had done so much research on how to release Keiko, Ken redirected to the fight to release Lolita. Howard eventually took over his efforts. "She was a far better candidate for release anyway, because we know her family, and they are easy to find," he shared.

Her campaign continues, over two decades later. Lolita has been stuck in a bureaucratic nightmare that at times seems hopeless and at other times on the edge of a breakthrough. Whatever its status, Howard, on behalf of Orca Network, keeps interested parties informed. Orca Network, the nonprofit organization Howard cofounded with Susan Berta in 2001, evolved out of the Lolita campaign that he took over.

His hoped-for prize for all those years spent campaigning for her release and operating the organization is her "coming home," Howard stated. "I think it would elevate our understanding and our fascination with orcas beyond anything to date." But even if Lolita doesn't get released, he knows all that effort wasn't for naught. "Just to tell her story and to explain why we're optimistic that she could make that change is rewarding. For people to understand that she has the capability and strength and reserve and adaptability and memory—that she knows where she grew up and who her family is to this day—that's what's most important."

Having been captured in August of 1970, at the time of print, Lolita has been in captivity for almost forty-eight years—nearly all her life. That fact doesn't lower Howard's confidence that she can survive in the wild under the right rehabilitation plan—or at the very least be transferred to a permanent sea pen, which would be a massive upgrade from the conditions she's currently kept in. In a sea pen, she'd have a much larger area to exercise and swim, a natural and healthier habitat, greater stimulation, and protection from the blazing hot sun she is exposed to in Miami's shallow pool.

"Being able to tell her story is really impressive," Howard shared. Then again, he loves storytelling. Thankfully, his audience is getting wider and wider. Orca Network began in 2001 with about one hundred people on a contact list. Now, in 2018, that number is closer to fifteen thousand. Lolita's story is being heard, largely because of a hardcore group of individuals who are voicing their concerns to the parties who need to hear it: the owner of the Miami Seaquarium, the media, politicians, and people lined up to buy tickets to marine parks that hold whales and dolphins captive.

Progress may seem slow and uninspiring, but there has been progress nonetheless. Public attitude has shifted considerably since the day of Lolita's capture in Penn Cove, off Whidbey Island, Washington. Thanks to movies such as *Blackfish*, for which Howard was interviewed, a new wave of supporters is rallying behind the idea of releasing captive whales into sea pens (also known as sanctuaries) and keeping other whales and dolphins from being captured.

Howard said, "Awareness has grown exponentially with social media. Now there's many, many Facebook pages and petitions for Lolita and other captive marine mammals, and big events, and weekly demonstrations at the Seaquarium. All of that's purely spontaneous; we're not directing any of that. We're in touch and we cheerlead, but it's not our doing. So that's great—the campaign has taken off."

Orca Network does a lot more than campaign for the release of Lolita. The organization acts as a hub where people can stay informed about the current state of the endangered Southern Resident orca population as well as sightings of orcas and other whales and dolphins that visit Pacific Northwest waters. Regular emails and social media posts keep followers informed of recent whale births and deaths as well as upcoming events and opportunities to educate and inform both themselves and others.

The organization also gives talks at events and to audiences that include journalists, educators, law-makers and policy-makers, and the general public. As a result of their efforts, Howard said, "there is this ring of people that are eager to go see whales whenever they hear about them. Sometimes it's the same people coming out, but every time there are new people too, wanting to see them and talk to the people that are out there." Howard described Orca Network as simply being "the watering hole, where a lot of people want to come drink."

Of course, he understands the attraction—or in some cases, the healthy addiction—that leads people to stop whatever they're doing to put on their shoes (and sometimes an abundance of winter and rainproof gear) and go follow up on the latest sighting. "Whales are universal mood lifters." Howard smiled. "Nondenominational, nonpartisan, nonpharmaceutical, eagerly shared mood lifters. That's just how whales affect people." He paused before adding, "And me too."

Visit www.orcanetwork.org *for more information on educational events hosted by Orca Network, the campaign to release Lolita from captivity, and a detailed account of Keiko's life story, as told by Howard Garrett.* Photo by Jill Hein.

II
Captivity

Without knowledge and understanding of the complex social structures and high level of intelligence that cetaceans possess, it may seem perfectly acceptable to place them in aquariums for human entertainment (or what some parks like to call "education"). Audiences are taught that these animals are "friends of mankind" who enjoy "playing" with people. Although there may be unique situations where cetaceans in the wild seek out human interactions, those cases are unusual and on a very different level when initiated by wildlife itself.

For proponents of captivity, arguments are made that dolphins appear to be "smiling" even in captivity and orcas and belugas seem to have formed friendships with their theme park trainers. Sadly, there is a lot of misinformation out there about the appropriateness of keeping these animals in captivity. Dolphins only appear to smile—that is an anatomical illusion arising from the configuration of their jaws; to be a highly social animal kept in isolation results in a desperation for attention and stimulation that may falsely appear as friendship.

Although there is no recorded incident of an orca in the wild ever harming a human, there are several cases of orcas in captivity harming and even killing their trainers. Driven mad by their circumstances, they occasionally lash out, and that should be of no surprise to anyone. They have been separated from their families to be kept in tanks that are the equivalent of bathtubs and starved to the point where they'll accept dead fish (which is not their natural diet) in exchange for performing a few tricks, for the rest of their lives.

If we want to find a bright side in all of that, it would be that before orcas were seen in captivity beginning in 1964, they were widely perceived to be fierce and dangerous to humans and were shot and slaughtered in some countries. They still are harassed and killed by some fishermen—two orcas were harpooned in 2017 off the Caribbean island of St. Vincent in front of tourists on a whale watching boat, for example—and as previously told, they *can* be dangerous to humans in captivity. However, overall, there is an awareness and appreciation for the animal that was not seen prior to captive-based research.

Researchers have uncovered the orca's incredible ability to feel emotions, to solve complex problems, and to communicate in ways we couldn't previously imagine. Marine parks would have the public believe that such research is necessary to justify keeping whales and dolphins in captivity, but aside from a few studies on anatomy and physiology that could be applied to wild animals, how relevant are studies on behavior if conducted under such unusual circumstances? Floating, for example, is a captive-learned behavior that whales revert to out of boredom; boredom does not occur in the wild.

What's really impressive about cetaceans—their social structures and practices, migration patterns, hunting techniques, etc.—is not observable in captivity. Perhaps we have learned all we can objectively learn about whales and dolphins within such constraints, and aquariums would be better off admitting so. It is time to adopt a new cultural perspective—one that offers equal respect to the physical and emotional needs of intelligent animals as it does to people. Such a shift could be a powerful demonstration of the intelligence of humans.

There are, thankfully, many movements to treat those animals already in captivity with more dignity and respect and to eliminate the further capture and transport of wild animals, as well as the practice of breeding in captivity. Whale and Dolphin Conservation (WDC) lists efforts taking place in the following categories:

• Creating sea sanctuaries where whales and dolphins currently in captivity can be relocated to live more natural lives

- Stopping airlines from transporting whales and dolphins from Japanese drive hunts (small boats are used to drive the mammals into coves where they are killed) to aquatic parks
- Pressuring governments to ban the capture of whales and dolphins in the wild
- Increasing public awareness of welfare issues and cruelty associated with breeding in captivity
- Campaigning to stop tour operators from promoting shows that hold whales and dolphins in captivity
- Raising awareness among individuals that by buying a ticket to a marine park, they are supporting an industry that practices animal cruelty

Due to the efforts of many crusaders to educate future generations, there is reason to be hopeful that using intelligent animals for captive entertainment is soon to be a practice of the past.

ROSIE CAYOU-JAMES: *Our Orca Ancestors*

Rosie Cayou-James can captivate an audience without the use of words. She is a powerful storyteller, but it is her presence that draws people in first. Her movements are thoughtful, like the words she carefully selects and delivers. When she looks at you, you have the feeling she is looking straight into your soul. It is how one might describe what it's like to look into the eye of a whale.

It cannot be denied that, like orcas are, Rosie is a keeper of great wisdom. It is a wisdom that has been cultivated from her own life experiences and the experiences of her elders that have been passed on to her. Not all of those stories can be told, however. In some cases, she must first determine if an audience is worthy; in others, she must ask herself if the story is hers to tell.

Those who have the opportunity to hear her speak—whether it be through outreach she conducts on behalf of the Samish Indian Nation or through various events hosted by Orca Network—have been offered a unique honor. To listen to her stories about the orcas is to learn about the history of her people.

Rosie's father kept some stories secret, even from his daughter. He didn't open up to her about just how much the orcas meant to him until the day he lost some of them. That day was August 8, 1970. Eighty orcas were herded into Penn Cove off Whidbey Island, Washington. Six whales were captured, and five additional were killed in the process. Rosie and her father were there to witness what her father called an "abduction."

She shared her story: "To see those whales being hoisted up like that...to see parts of their fins or tails sticking out of those nets...To my dad, it was like watching his own children being kidnapped. He said that aside from losing our land, losing his family—the orcas—was the most devastating time in his life."

Her father, sitting on the beach inside the cove that day, apologized to the whales in his native language. He told them that he didn't know where they were taking them, but he promised to go there and get them back. "That never happened," Rosie lamented. Her father passed before anything could be done, but she has taken up his fight.

Tokitae, also known as Lolita, is the last surviving orca from the Puget Sound captures in the 1960s and '70s. She is being held at Miami Seaquarium, where she still performs daily. Rosie crusades for her release, using storytelling as a means to raise public awareness regarding the cruelty of captivity. "If that tank is their home, that tank is their toilet. And they've got to swim in it. That is inhumane," she said.

Captivity is not the only concern she has for the whales. For her beloved Southern Resident killer whales, it's the dwindling supply of salmon. "As humans, we are spoiled," she began. "We can go out and buy anything we want to eat, and many times that's salmon." She paused for emphasis before continuing, "Meanwhile, our family of orcas are starving to death."

And it's not just the orcas who are hungry—it's gray whales too. In April of 2010, Rosie received a call from Orca Network's Howard Garrett and Susan Berta. There was a deceased gray whale beached on Samish Island, and they were wondering if she and her partner, Tsulton, could go over and help "feed the spirit of the whale." The whale had been attempting to feed in the sand before she died.

"We went out there, but we couldn't find anywhere without a 'no trespassing' sign on the island that we once owned," Rosie remarked. "We drove around until we pulled over in a little grassy area. We knew we were going to get approached and probably kicked off. A man came down to see what we were doing, but when we told him, he said, 'You are welcome.' We walked a good mile until we could reach the whale."

The couple performed their ceremony. "Tsulton went out there and gently captured her spirit. She wanted to come to him; she didn't know what direction to go. He turned around toward the ocean, and he let her spirit go. He had tears; he was shaking his head. I asked him if there was anything I could do, and he said, 'No, she's fine now. Her family fed her. Her spirit was starving for its natural food, but it could only find one shrimp."

When the whale was later dissected, only one sand shrimp was found in her stomach. The rest was sawdust. There had been a sawmill at the location many years ago, and the sediment in the area was still polluted with its remains.

Although Rosie realized the gravity of the situation, she didn't allow herself to get caught up in despair. Her humor prevailed: "I wish we had a food bank for the whales...over at that bank there's shrimp for the gray whales, and over at that bank there's salmon for the Residents." She chuckled before her tone turned more serious.

"At some point I would like to reach out to fishermen to ask—and this is a big request, but it's for the future of both whales and humans—that they don't set nets in the water for four years. That's what orcas mean to me. Because without salmon, the Resident orcas are going to die, and the seals are going to die. And without seals, the Transient orcas could die."

That experience of feeding the gray whale's spirit led Orca Network to ask the couple to conduct an annual ceremony on the anniversary of the Penn Cove captures. Every August 8 from the Coupeville, Washington, dock, Rosie, Tsulton, and members of the concerned public feed the spirit of the orcas who were captured and those who died. Salmon is laid on a bed of cedar branches and allowed to drift out to sea as songs and stories are shared.

Rosie has undertaken other means to help feed and free the orcas. She is active in efforts to promote salmon habitat restoration, and she advocates for whale watching in the wild versus in captivity. She is hopeful about the future. "I think that the public is catching on. Now, if they want to see a whale, they want to see them in their natural habitat. Instead of flying to Florida for SeaWorld, people are taking the time to come up here and look off a bank or go out on a whale watching boat."

After working at the Samish Nation for fifteen years and through all of her presentations, she has witnessed this shift in public perception. "There's a core group of people in every town who are going to keep reeling in more people. Just as I do with my storytelling, people are reeling other people in by using emotion. When I give a workshop, I see a lot of tears, so I know people are starting to get in tune with their spirit. Maybe some of their spirit guides are orca, or maybe they're gray whale."

Rosie's spirit guide is definitely an orca. One of the presentations she does is called "My Life as an Orca." She lets the spirit of the orca guide her into conversation that reveals the life story of her as an orca, from learning how to catch her first food to how to scratch her tummy. "I never know what's going to come out of me. It's different every time." She smiles. Her love for storytelling is adamant in the joy that spreads across her face. Her passion is sensed and spread to her audience. Listeners get goosebumps as she tells her stories.

Despite having grown up with stories of orcas as spirit guides and amiable to humans, Rosie's first reaction to seeing an orca in the wild was one of mixed emotions. "The orca was going between a reef and an island, probably about two hundred yards off the beach. It was chilling and exciting at the same time. I didn't know whether to laugh from happiness or cry from fear." She glowed at the memory.

She also remembered a time out fishing with her father; he caught a sixty-pound salmon near Deception Pass, toward the mouth of the Skagit River. "My father said, 'Well, the orcas are on their way, because this one is wild.' And sure enough, there came the orcas." She let out a small squeal, reliving the moment.

On another occasion, Rosie was out on the water when she stopped to sing a song for the orcas. The family of orcas known as J-pod showed up with Granny, the matriarch, breaching beside the boat. "They have such sensitive hearing," she shared. "Dad had told me they could hear him sing from one hundred miles away, and that's how I knew it was true." Despite many close encounters, she had never been quite as close to the orcas as her father had been. "I never made eye contact with whales like my father. I can only see through his eyes what that must be like."

All of Rosie's memories of the orcas are sentimental, regarded as "more priceless than gold." They are what fuel her passion for their protection. "Their safety is real important to me. If the whales here went extinct, there would be a lot of grief. Like any other family member, we'd have to hold onto the memories."

She concluded, "Orcas are the other half of my life. They're the other half of my tribe's life. Some people don't look at our relationship to the orcas that way anymore, but I still do because of the stories that I was raised with. My dad was born on Orcas Island. His best friends were orcas. When he traveled from island to island, he had friends along the way. His having had the spirit of orcas to guide him through life has been passed on to me."

Visit www.samishtribe.nsn.us *to learn more about the Samish Indian Nation.*

KATIE EMMONS AND ABBIE EMMONS: *Voices for the Voiceless*

Katie and Abbie Emmons not only share the same outside-the-box thinking and concern for wildlife and the environment, they share the same blood. The sisters were raised together, homeschooled together, and inspired to create a film together to raise awareness about the cruelty of keeping orcas and dolphins in captivity. What makes their film unique is that it was made by students, for students.

Although they are in their early twenties now, as teenagers, the young women understood that the generation holding the key to ending captivity was their own; children and teens were the people pleading with their parents for tickets to marine parks, so they had to be the ones to choose to stop visiting those places. Filming for *Voiceless* began in 2012, a Kickstarter campaign was launched and successfully funded in 2014, and the documentary subsequently premiered at Superpod, the annual gathering of orca enthusiasts on San Juan Island, Washington, in July of 2016. The thirty-minute film is currently available on YouTube for free.

Millennials often get labeled as "self-absorbed slackers." Katie and Abbie demonstrate how misleading that reputation can be. Having forgone the college route, the two are now writers, activists, and cofounders of the nonprofit organization Blue Freedom. Their paths may not be traditional ones, but they have accomplished more in their young lives than many multi-degree-laden older adults. By example, they have shown that young people can and do have a voice—and that it can be used to "give a voice to the voiceless."

Having grown up in Vermont—the only New England state without a coastline—Katie and Abbie somehow still have long felt an affinity for the ocean. Their love for marine mammals grew out of their broad love for all animals. Their education was largely self-directed; if one of them showed an interest in a subject, both sisters were encouraged to further explore it. They asked to study the ocean.

Their mother was their main teacher, but they also had guest tutors. The flexible structure of their schooling is something the sisters feel very lucky to have been offered. "We were able to delve into environmental topics that otherwise might have been pushed aside," Katie explained. "We did endangered species studies and oceanography studies. We read the whole history of whaling."

Aside from their formal education, the sisters were raised with early exposure to the concept of conservation. Katie continued, "Our family is very environmentally conscientious. We were raised to look at our impact on earth—on people, the environment, animals, plants—and also what larger actions we could take to support it." At first, those actions consisted of donating to the local animal shelter and adopting pets of their own. But as the sisters grew older, larger actions came to mind.

The impetus for creating a film about cetaceans was their viewing of another film on the topic: *The Cove*. The 2010 Academy Award–winning documentary brought to light the cruelty of dolphin hunting practices in Taiji, Japan. Though the two were familiar with factory farming and the slaughter of various land animals, they had previously never heard of dolphin slaughter. "I was around fourteen when the film came out, and it blew me away," Katie shared. "I thought, even though I'm just a teenager, there has to be something I can do to raise awareness about this." Abbie agreed.

The sisters created a website and began blogging about the issue of dolphins and orcas in captivity. Abbie and Katie realized they'd had ties to a rather famous captive orca when they were only one and three years old, respectively. Their parents had taken them to the Oregon Coast Aquarium while Keiko—the star of *Free Willy*—was there in rehabilitation, preparing for release back into the wild. "Even back then, there were hints as to where our journey would lead." Katie smiled. Their research also made them aware of another soon-to-be-famous orca.

After interviewing former SeaWorld trainers who had formed the collective Voice of the Orcas, the sisters became inspired to help Tilikum, an orca held in captivity at SeaWorld in Orlando, Florida. They began a petition for his release, just before another whale film, *Blackfish*, took the world by storm. The 2013 documentary film featured Tilikum and the suffering he'd endured in captivity. After the film premiered at the Sundance Film Festival, it was subsequently picked up for wider release by CNN Films. Google flooded with searches for "how to help Tilikum."

Katie and Abbie's petition was the first link that appeared. "We ended up getting over two hundred thousand signatures. It snowballed from there," Katie stated. They instantly recognized the power of film, but it was their father who suggested they make their own—a film by students, he explained, would help young people resonate with their message.

The biggest obstacle was funding. Katie and Abbie used the Kickstarter platform to raise money for the film. Their blog readers and social media followers stepped up. "It really inspired us to see how much our supporters believed in us," Katie shared. Their goal was to raise $17,000 by the end of their sixty-day campaign. They ended up raising $22,000 in five days. "We never expected that. Our campaign jumped to the number one trending spot on Kickstarter. People obviously wanted us to make this film."

The sisters became certain they could make a difference, even as teenagers. Katie detailed: "In the sphere of environmentalism, there's a general vibe that if you want to help you have to get into the sciences, which really isn't the case. There are so many creative ways to raise awareness, and art and film is really what filters into the mainstream—it's not the raw data. Stories communicate data better than science."

Via their film, Katie and Abbie took the story of Tilikum and other captive orcas and dolphins into classrooms. They held Q&A discussions with classes all over the world. Katie shared, "I did a Skype-in session with a school in Barcelona, Spain, where I could see the whole classroom. I talked to them about the documentary and whales and what they could do to make a difference. So many students have the perception that because they're young there's nothing they can do, so I chatted with them about what I did as a teenager, while the teacher translated."

Katie has done the same with classrooms in the Netherlands, Italy, and Turkey—the latter was restricted to a chat session and email correspondence, to more easily overcome the language barrier. Local classroom initiatives have been harder to come by. "It's difficult in the States to figure out how to contact schools, but the film has opened up discussions with educators, and I've been able to see just how many are interested in the subject."

The film also opened up opportunities for the young women to educate through speaker panels. One of the largest events they participated in was a symposium held in Rochester, New York, which they then featured briefly at the end of their film. Their presence at Superpod on San Juan Island was another highlight. Katie detailed, "We were on a panel with Lori Marino, Ingrid Visser, and Naomi Rose, so that was a surreal opportunity to mingle with these world-renowned scientists and researchers. I remember being nine years old and reading *All Animals* magazine, cutting out clips of Naomi Rose's articles about whales, and here I was sitting on a panel with her!"

Their passion and commitment are all the more amazing because Katie and Abbie did not see orcas in the wild until after they finished their film and were attending Superpod. While whale watching on the island, they saw a pod of orcas. Katie described the experience: "It was surreal to see how massive they are. But then I was overcome with sadness for the animals in captivity because I knew that's what they should be experiencing too. It was bittersweet, but it only created more motivation to help the public understand that's how these animals are supposed to live."

Abbie chimed in: "It was a visceral experience, to see the mammal I'd spent so many years studying and thinking about how to serve. Finally, I was witnessing what I was fighting for and what was constantly driving me. Seeing those whales in their natural habitat, doing what they're meant to do...it was incredible to see firsthand what I do all this volunteer work for."

Everything the sisters do for the orcas is volunteer service. All funds that come in to Blue Freedom go toward distributing the film or the traveling to get to an event in support of the film. Katie and Abbie drive home that lack of funds should never be a deterrent to pursuing one's passion—there are creative ways to fund any goal. "You could have a business that produces products such as books and T-shirts that raise awareness for your cause but also support you so you can do the work," Katie offered as an example.

Katie and Abbie agree that fear of negative feedback also should not be an impediment to addressing controversial subjects. Although messages of positive feedback highly outnumber the negative, they do occasionally face criticism from individuals who support captivity institutions. "We mostly just ignore the negative feedback." Katie laughed. "Although sometimes we get emails from people who ask us to further explain why captivity is bad. If they are open-minded, we always take the time to discuss the issue further with them."

In any case, the young women focus on the positive—not just in regard to their own feedback but the level of public awareness for their cause in general. "So many books and films are starting to slowly make a change, so seeing that shift is what encourages us to keep going." In validation of Katie's optimism, Blue Freedom's support base continues to grow, with a surprising number of people from the United Kingdom and Europe. "There are a lot of anticaptivity initiatives overseas," Katie explained.

Leading many of those initiatives are young people, just like Katie and Abbie. "Millennials have so much to offer," Katie began. "A lot of people say, 'Kids these days, all they want to do is play online all day,' but a lot of kids don't do anything because they have an underlying belief that there's nothing they can do at their age, but that's not true. Everyone has a role to play. With social media and where we are technologically today, we have a greater capacity than ever before to spread information."

Her advice to young people is the following: "Whatever you want to undertake as far as schooling or a career, go for it—but know that you don't need anything other than your laptop to raise awareness for an issue you care about." If marine mammals are one's passion, Katie reminds younger and older people alike that you don't have to drop everything and become a marine biologist. "If you're a writer, write books. If you're into film editing, make films. If you draw or do photography, use those as tools to help convey your message."

Nor does one have to move to a location close to the sea. In fact, the sisters partially attribute their quick thinking to having grown up in their small, noncoastal Vermont town. "Vermont is such a unique little spot, an incubator for environmental and humanitarian causes." Even if a person's local community doesn't have a network of like-minded people, Katie pointed out that the internet can introduce people to powerful networks of supporters. "You can find your community online and then go to events through that network to continue building that community."

Their unconventional education was the other major catalyst for their large-scale ambition. "Being homeschooled nurtured a lot of our environmental passion and gave us the time and space to get involved in extracurricular endeavors. All of our homeschooled friends tend to be involved in some cause or another," Katie said.

Katie and Abbie are likely to get involved in other causes themselves and perhaps even create another film. "When you start interviewing people in the environmental field, there are so many story ideas that start popping up," Katie said. "We definitely keep the thought of doing another film in the back of our minds."

This time, they may not need to hire a film company. Abbie's film-editing skills have evolved significantly since they created their first film. She shared, "*Voiceless* opened up new ways for me to think about filmmaking. And it brought to my attention how much of an impact artistic forms can have in regard to spreading awareness about a subject."

Find out more about the nonprofit organization Blue Freedom and watch the film Voiceless *online at* www.bluefreedom.org.

CLIVE MARTIN: *Sea Sanctuaries for Cetaceans*

Although he much prefers the company of wildlife over people, Clive Martin seems to make new friends wherever he goes. His British accent attracts attention on its own, but it's the humor and humility behind his words that draw people to him. Though there is a natural interplay that occurs between Clive and everyone from strangers in a bar to his audiences at presentations, the relationships that drive him are passive ones: between him and wild animals.

He is one of the founding members of the World Cetacean Alliance, which was born of his desire for conservation groups to collaborate rather than compete. For nearly two decades, he has been working tirelessly to educate people aboard cruise ships about the magnificence of cetaceans and the threats facing them and to put an end to the practice of captivity.

As a master organizer, visionary, and passion-driven man, he is capable of helping make the latter possible. Through the creation of the Orca Rescues Foundation, Clive's fund-raising efforts are helping to facilitate the rescue and rehabilitation of orca and dolphins in captivity.

He has recently teamed up with fellow specialists in Greece and around the globe to help bring the Aegean Marine Life Sanctuary to life, which is on track to become the first sanctuary in the world for stranded, injured, and formerly exploited dolphins.

Clive wasn't often grounded as a child, but when he was, he didn't mind. He was born with an insatiable curiosity for wildlife, and confinement to his room was exactly what he needed in order to indulge in his passion. Tucked quietly under the bed covers, he would read *The Observer's Book of Wild Animals* by flashlight, soaking up everything he could about the species that resided in and around his home of New Forest, in southern England.

He ruled out most education and career paths—including his initial interest in becoming a veterinary surgeon—on account of his self-proclaimed lack of academic dexterity. He knew he had to pick some profession, however, and his organizational skills landed him in the hotel and tourism industry. After four years of training, he quickly worked his way up to the position of operations director for a large hotel group based on the south coast of the United Kingdom.

When he needed to unwind from the busy commercial world, Clive knew just what to do. He rallied his dogs and went for a stroll through nature. "We'd follow a herd of wild deer and simply sit and observe them. It was the same with foxes, badgers, otters...I would find all these spots that became my solace away." Despite wanting to be close to them, he didn't want to feed them or alter their experience in any way; he innately understood that nature needed to be kept natural.

By 1995 he had become well-versed in land mammals but had very little knowledge of cetaceans—he had never even heard the word. An invitation from his daughter to attend a course about dolphins on the Welsh coast changed all that. The course was taught by a marine scientist who was setting up a coastal network for marine mammal observation. When he learned of Clive's administrative background, he eagerly suggested Clive become involved with the project.

The Biscay Dolphin Research Programme had no funds, and the team had no idea how to administer the organization. Clive was intrigued by the suggestion but instead worked another four years in hotel management before a serious fall from a ladder in 1999 led him to contemplate his direction in life. After nine months in a hospital bed and relearning how to walk, Clive knew what he had to do: accept the offer to do something he considered more meaningful with his life. He became the director of the Biscay Dolphin Research Programme.

The organization's home was on a working cruise ship, *The Pride of Bilbao*, whose route was Portsmouth, England, through the Bay of Biscay to Bilbao, Spain. The bay used to be known for its storms, but as a result of the research program's efforts, it is now also known as a prime whale watching region.

Rather than stay separated from the cruise guests, Clive suggested the organization take advantage of the built-in audience. With the cruise director's support, they started offering educational presentations, accepting donations for them, and selling merchandise in the ship's gift shop. Before long, word spread that the three-day cruise offered an incredible whale and dolphin experience.

It soon became obvious that whale enthusiasts were filling the ships, eager to see the thirty-one species of cetaceans the research team had identified. Clive came to perfect his top-deck presentation; he mapped the length of blue, fin, and pilot whales on the massive ship and put together an identification board showing each species that had been seen in the area. His deck whale watches drew lots of curious passengers. "Due to the symbiosis of my organization and the cruise route, I was able to conduct research on what species were sighted, how many babies and juveniles were seen, the weather conditions and all sorts of factors that we scientifically took into account," Clive said.

The team grew to include trained marine mammal observers, and the organization's knowledge grew too. One critical threat to whales shocked them: navy sonar and oil exploration sound guns confused beaked whales so much that they would swim toward land and become stranded on beaches. Once the navy owned up to their responsibility, they agreed to work with the research team's marine mammal observers to not fire sonar or sound guns if whales or dolphins were sighted in the area. Since the researchers knew the species most affected by sound, they also knew where to spot them: near the big continental shelf slopes. The program therefore played a critical role in not only research and education but marine mammal protection.

One of Clive's more remarkable whale watching experiences was one in which he was able to protect a female humpback and her calf, not from the military but from two overly enthusiastic male suitors. After spotting a great deal of water eruption about ten miles ahead of the ship, Clive gave running commentary to the passengers about what was happening, and that to ensure that the ship did not intrude on the encounter, a slow pass-by would be made. Clive recalled, "At the closest point we got to them, the female suddenly let out a very large 'bellow,' an acoustic reaction I had never heard in a whale before or since. I think we helped her out, as the males became less enthusiastic with their mating desires and eased up on their intentions."

After Clive served fifteen years as a researcher and naturalist aboard the ship, the cruise company ended that particular route, and the Biscay Dolphin Research Programme was forced to end along with it. Clive was ready for the change. "My ship had literally gone. It was an organic move," he concluded.

Official research through the program may have ended, but Clive's work in the field did not. He knew he couldn't go back to working for someone else—he had "to have autonomy and live and breathe by my own mistakes and successes." Therefore, he went on to create his own company. As a guest entertainer aboard Carnival cruise ships, he delivers introductory presentations on whales, dolphins, and other sea life—and he's training a small team of individuals so that multiple cruise routes can be taken on at a time.

Clive doesn't consider himself an educator, but he's educated thousands of people about the world's oceans and helped them to understand the pressures human activity places on marine life. Aside from his ship talks, he has given a presentation to the European Union Commissioner of Fisheries and Agriculture about the number of dolphins caught in bycatch (the term given to unwanted fish or other marine life caught while commercially fishing for another species), been featured on Spanish TV for his work with the Biscay Dolphin Research Programme, and given a radio presentation in Belize.

The latter was done to ensure that the country's representative to the International Whaling Commission (IWC) would participate in a crucial vote to maintain the moratorium on whaling, which had been declared in 1984. Belize needed the public to support the representative's participation so that the government would fund his travel to the meeting. Thanks at least in part to Clive's radio talk, the citizens were informed and demanded representation at the vote. "Belize did attend the meeting, and the vote held!" Clive proudly declared. He concluded that sometimes the public just needs to be nudged in the right direction.

A recurring theme throughout Clive's career is his amazement at how few people realize what is going on with the world's oceans and the life they support. "The awareness people have regarding ocean litter has only begun to be discussed in recent years," he shared. "But we've been on about it for many years. I've traveled transatlantic many times; when we pass an ocean gyre and it's full of a football field of litter going around and around...you have to try and do something about it."

The amount of trash, particularly plastics, in the ocean is deeply disturbing to Clive. He recalled learning about a necropsy done on a Cuvier's beaked whale that uncovered thirty plastic bags and additional plastic items clogging the whale's stomach. The whale had stranded near Bergen, Norway, in 2017, emaciated and about to die. "Cuvier's beaked whales are suck feeders; they don't have teeth," Clive explained. "The sonar pulse that they get from a jellyfish is the same that's likely to come off a piece of polythene, so their brain says 'food,' and they suck it up." The whale has become known among media as "the plastic whale," but it is sadly not the first—and it won't be the last—to turn up with a stomach full of plastic.

Clive has repeatedly asked Carnival to stop using plastic straws on its ships, thus far to no avail. He explained, "Passengers are not allowed to take their glasses to the decks of the ships, so they're given plastic cups with plastic straws. People put their drink down, a little puff of wind comes, and, poof...more plastic in the ocean." Regardless of the lack of headway with management, he keeps fighting to educate the passengers.

He understands that firsthand experience with cetaceans can have a critical influence on their actions. "When people see their first dolphin or whale, they're so excited that words fail them. It's quite an emotional experience for them; they're in awe. But I don't think they understand what's going on with them." Being able to have the experience of seeing whales in the wild, however, sets them apart from many people who don't have access to field education.

"For marine scientists, 'in the field' means out on the ocean—the deep ocean. Many students today don't have access to that kind of education. How do they learn about these mammals, if they can't see them? They need a ship or a boat." Clive considers himself fortunate to be able to have had the education he's had—one that, interestingly, was not pursued through an institution but rather entirely through self-education. Everything he knows has come from reading countless books, attending conferences, and being out in the field.

One message he wants parents to focus on is that even though taking children out on whale watching trips may seem costly, taking them to marine parks is not an acceptable alternative educational resource. "So many people have been told downright lies by these so-called conservation and education institutions. They will tell their audiences and their trainers that orcas are long-lived at thirty, when in fact they can live to over one hundred in the wild. It suits their business to misrepresent the truth in that way," Clive said.

"You can educate your children in a better way," Clive suggests to parents. "You may have to save up a bit harder, but you can go whale watching pretty much anywhere in the world. You can buy books and put your kids in that trajectory. Don't go to marine parks. You don't know what's in the back of it." He said this to his passengers before the documentary film *Blackfish* came out—which was a catalyst for changing public opinion on cetacean captivity.

The film explained the emotional and physical damage done to orcas during captures and captivity and profiled attacks on human trainers committed by captive orcas, most notably two fatal attacks by the orca known as Tilikum. Clive shared, "What those trainers found out the very hard way is that you don't mess with wild animals. And SeaWorld and other marine parks are messing with them big time, to the point that human deaths have taken place."

Many captive orcas have gone psychopathic and even suicidal. The compilation of stressors of being held in tiny tanks with no shelter from the sun and only being fed if they performed tricks takes a toll on their bodies and minds. Tilikum passed away in January of 2017, but the suffering he endured wasn't entirely in vain. He served as a great inspiration to Clive and many other people who learned of his plight through the film.

"The best thing to help activists against captivity was *Blackfish*," he shared. "We were able to jump on the back of that film and really ramp up the whole captivity nonsense." He is aware of many organizations working toward the same goal of ending whaling and cetacean captivity, but in the end, he's had the foresight to understand that an appropriate plan and place has to exist before those remaining in captivity can get out. And that plan requires significant funding.

Putting his operational skills to good use, Clive founded Orca Rescues Foundation. The nonprofit organization's mission is "to establish a global fund to facilitate the release and rehabilitation back to the wild or near-wild of orca in captivity and to give support to specialists, scientists, and organizations working to achieve this." In other words, "our creed is to support the people in the frontline who are working to get these animals out of captivity and to make sure it doesn't progress."

One of these frontline groups is the Aegean Marine Life Sanctuary, situated on the Greek island of Lipsi. Although nine other dolphin sanctuaries are in various stages of development around the world, the Aegean sanctuary may become the first sanctuary in the world for dolphins rescued from captivity. Support for the organization is one of Orca Rescues Foundation's priorities.

Opponents of releasing captive orcas and dolphins most often do not understand the complexity of the planning undergone before such an act is considered. Clive does, however—and so does the solid team behind the Aegean Marine Life Sanctuary and other sea sanctuaries in development. "You can't just get a crane, put them in a sling, and dump them in an ocean," Clive stated. "They've got to be looked after."

In the case of the Aegean sanctuary, years of environmental surveys and logistical planning have already passed. "The rehabilitation process has to be extreme and very carefully planned," Clive explained. "We're wanting them to live a much better life as near to wild as possible, but it has to be done in the right way. Aside from Keiko [the star of *Free Willy* whose story was outlined earlier], this hasn't been done before. And with Keiko, lessons could be learned in order to have handled his release better—but at least he died free. If I were in prison for no reason whatsoever, would I rather die there or regain my freedom, even for a short time? I would choose to regain my freedom," Clive said.

To be done properly, a team of professionals needs to be assembled, so the sanctuary put together SEAS (Sanctuary Education and Advisory Specialists) to ensure the highest standards for rehabilitation and retirement into seminatural conditions for the dolphins. To prevent the transfer of diseases between captive dolphins and wild dolphins, the team will quarantine the newly released dolphins.

Then, the dolphins will be introduced to the sanctuary in phases. To reduce stress, their boundary will be moved farther and farther out over time. They will also be introduced to the other dolphins in the sanctuary in a slow and organic way.

The dolphins will be given the opportunity to relearn natural behaviors such as hunting for live fish, which will be supplied by local fishermen. "They still have their animal instincts," Clive purported. "Taken out of captivity, if you give them wild fish, they will catch them. They are intelligent beings." Over time, some of the dolphins may become good candidates for release into the wild, but those who were born into captivity will be unlikely to be released.

The team's goal is to phase in the opportunity for the public, especially those who are helping fund the project, to view the animals in the sanctuary. Initially, the sanctuary will focus on the rehabilitation of the animals and offer minimal human contact.

"They're used to seeing two hundred people gawking and laughing at them, so we can't suddenly eliminate human contact," Clive warned. "They will be hand-fed at first, but bit by bit they'll get to hunt fish. They will be ensured proper veterinary care throughout the process." The team's goal is to "get this template to perfection and create the gold standard" for sea sanctuaries, before introducing it to the public.

Clive is hoping that the sanctuary will demonstrate to people who have been proponents of captivity that using sentient beings for human entertainment is not OK and that whales are highly capable of readjusting to life in a natural setting. "Cetaceans are sentient in different ways than ourselves—they don't know their ABCs and such—but when you get the chance to observe them, you are in wonder of their behaviors and communication and their intelligence."

Clive's involvement with Orca Rescue Foundation and the sea sanctuary—combined with his Carnival cruise presentations—has developed to the extent that he's had to let go of other commitments in his life. Until recently, he served as a trustee for the World Cetacean Alliance, of which he was one of the founding members. The organization evolved out of a discussion at the first Whale Fest in Brighton, United Kingdom, in 2013, at which it was agreed that there should be more alliances built in the industry, rather than competition for funding and a protective nature around data.

The alliance has since grown to include around one hundred members from around the world, with representatives on every continent. "It's a young organization yet, but working collectively, it will become a strong organization," Clive said. "The alliance is now even about to be represented on the IWC."

The topic of whaling is, naturally, one that triggers Clive. "Everyone thinks it's over," he began. "It's not. People like to say, 'Those Japanese, they're terrible.' They're desperately guilty of it, certainly, but so is or has been every nation in the world, including Great Britain, the United States, and Canada. Don't just pick on one nation. A lot of people in Japan are very much against whaling and will be the ones in the future to stop it, so we have to work with those people instead of blaming them all the time."

One of the presentations Clive does on the cruise ships is about whaling—the history of it and where it is now. He likes to have people imagine what they might have seen one or two hundred years ago. "What was it like before we killed them?" he ponders. "What was the population of the Northern Pacific Right whale before humans piled into them? Why did we do that?"

Despite past and current human behaviors, Clive has reason to feel hope for the future. Inspiration was found, for example, in a four-year-old boy named William who was aboard one of the cruise ships. "He came up to me and asked me about Megladon, a prehistoric shark. I had never met a four-year old that contemplated Megladon before. What's he going to turn out to be? We need to give him and all kids every bit of help we can."

Inspiring and supporting the next generation is a responsibility he takes seriously. "If there's anything I can do in my stage of life to try and bring forward what will be the excellence of the future, I will do it. I want them to flourish and to continue to do this work when I am no longer able." When asked what advice he would give to the younger generation contemplating a career with marine mammals, his energy elevated and his words flowed from the heart:

"Don't let anybody put you off. Understand that environmental science is not desperately well paid, but don't let that put you off either. There are opportunities for you to make a living. But get the advice of people who are in the trade—go to the student places that are at every single whale and environmental conservation conference. Learn where those conferences are and find the funding to get you there. Be a volunteer, help serve the teas and coffees, network. It's the direct eyeball to eyeball contact that's so important. I never got a job from writing a CV; I got it from people who knew me.

"And read about everything you can—not just about cetaceans but how they fit into everything else that's in the ocean: the currents, plankton, sand, rocks, tides, turtles, bellfish, sharks, and so forth. You have to try and get an all-encompassing view of the whole ecosystem. Don't expect anything to come to you on a silver platter, because it won't." Lest any reader get discouraged by his advice, Clive added, "But that's all achievable. It's like climbing a ladder. You get up three rungs and are forced down. There's always something knocking you down, but just remain on your path. You will climb up a little higher the next time."

Clive has no idea how many lives he has influenced over the years, but considering all of the people he's spoken to through his presentations, it's likely to be a far greater number than he imagines. He confided the following: "I would like to leave this planet thinking I just might have helped a smidgeon. Then I will think, 'OK, I can rest easy.'"

In a humble afterthought, Clive shared that there was one person whose life he may not have simply influenced but in fact saved. As a volunteer for a charity called the Royal National Lifeboat Institution (RNLI), Clive was at the lifeboat's helm when the coastguard informed him that a seriously injured man, who had fallen from a two-hundred-foot cliff onto a remote beach in Cornwall, needed to be rescued.

"Unfortunately," Clive said, "our way into the beach was strewn with jagged rocks and heavy swells of the North Coast Cornish kind!" Clive managed to guide the boat and the crew to the beach, however, and with great care got the man into the lifeboat and to a hospital. In recognition of his effort, Clive was awarded an honor called a vellum, which was signed by the president of the RNLI and Edward, the Duke of Kent. Clive should, indeed, think he can rest easy.

Although Clive considers himself retired, he clearly is still working hard. It doesn't feel like work, though, because he's now able to focus solely on what he loves to do: educating people on cruise ships. "I can enjoy my moments of glory when the people smile because I've showed them their first whale...and that's all I need now."

His jovial nature supports his declaration that he's the happiest he's been in his life, most likely a result of all the time he has to observe wildlife. "If you were to ask me what I get out of it, or if I can describe the feeling I get working with dolphins and whales, that's very difficult to answer. It's something from within, and I get exactly the same feeling when I am close to any one animal." Perhaps one animal in particular. "When I see a sperm whale, I'm in awe. I stop talking. It's my whale. I'm not going to tell you about it." He laughed.

Out of all the emotions he has experienced while watching cetaceans, there is one Clive has never exhibited—although he might someday soon. "I've never shed a tear for a dolphin or whale in my life. Hard man. But if I can stand at the sanctuary in the Aegean Sea, looking out at that pristine bit of habitat and see dolphins out there...I think I would cry."

To learn more about Orca Rescues Foundation, visit www.orcarescues.org. *More information on the Aegean Marine Life Sanctuary can be found at* http://archipelago.gr/en/. Photo by Jo-Blaise Martin.

III
ETHICAL EDUCATION

Although not always the most accessible, alternatives to visiting theme parks are abundant. A lot can be learned about the amazing cetacean—much more accurate and far-reaching information—by observing them in their natural habitats. Whale watching as an industry is booming in many coastal communities worldwide and is estimated to generate $2 billion annually. It is a much more lucrative business than whaling and one that supports developing economies and provides local employment.

There is cause for concern that the whale watching industry has grown too much too quickly; so many boats on the water can be detrimental to whales and dolphins. However, compared to keeping and observing whales in captivity, whale watching is certainly preferable. In general, shore-based whale watching is recommended as the least obtrusive form of getting to know these incredible creatures without negatively influencing their daily lives.

Resources are available in the back of this book for those wishing to support organizations or efforts to end cetacean captivity. In addition, guidelines help you select whale watching companies that operate ethically and responsibly as well as locate some of the best shore-based whale watching sites. Patience is required for those who choose the latter, but the reward is much sweeter.

The fact that millions of people forego opportunities to observe whales in their natural habitats and instead opt to buy tickets for guaranteed sightings at marine parks says a lot about the state of modern human culture. We don't want to have to wait for anything. We crave instant gratification and we want guaranteed success. Whales make no promises about where they're going to be any given day. Human vacation time, however, is most likely limited.

If a family lives in an inland state, it can be an expensive trip to the coast. But bringing children to theme parks—including zoos—isn't exactly the most educational experience to offer them. Children would learn more, and probably have more fun, going camping. Maybe they won't see a whale, but they will cultivate a hands-on relationship with nature—and every animal and aspect of nature is part of the same ecosystem, after all.

An alternative to both sea- and shore-based whale watching is visiting museums. Many inland and coastal states alike are migrating toward virtual reality experiences where visitors get the sensation they are swimming underwater with whales and dolphins. Many museums offer the less technologically advanced but nonetheless stunning experience of seeing real whale skeletons. For those readers living near coastal areas, volunteering for marine mammal stranding networks may even open up opportunities to clean beached whale carcasses for educational display. It's a smelly job, but someone has to do it.

BOB OTIS: *Studying from Shore*

Bob Otis has been studying orcas for twenty-eight years. Almost as long as he's been studying people. As a professor emeritus of psychology, he also studies people who watch whales. These two observations offer a parallel sense of wonder that, even as a researcher, he feels can't be scientifically explained given the resources we have today.

His first reaction to seeing whales can't be logically or verbally explained either. Nor can the wild trajectory that led him from one point to another in life. But he can ascertain that he got to where he is by saying yes to opportunities that made him feel good. Observing orcas in the wild made him feel good—again and again and again.

Every year since 1990, from May 20 to August 10, between the hours of 9:00 a.m. and 5:00 p.m., Bob has positioned himself at the Lime Kiln Lighthouse on San Juan Island, Washington. With his team of interns from Ripon College in Wisconsin and universities around the world, he observes and records the behaviors of every orca that passes by the lighthouse. The team focuses attention on factors that may pose a threat to the orcas—food supply, boats, aircraft (including drones), and so forth.

Known as one of the best shore-based whale watching spots in the world, the location is rife with opportunities to simultaneously observe the variety of comical, emotional, and universal reactions of over three hundred fifty thousand visitors from over forty countries who annually visit the site. Bob has seen it all...and he keeps coming back for more.

At first blush, Bob seems an unlikely candidate to conduct nearly three decades of marine mammal research on a Washington island. After all, for nine months out of the year, he runs a small farm in Wisconsin. But dig deeper and there are telltale signs that he was made to do what he does.

The first clue is the fact that he grew up only about fifty miles east of the island, in Bellingham, Washington. The second is that he's always had a fascination with animal behavior; even as an undergraduate at Western Washington University, he taught behavior labs. The third clue is that he went on to become a professor of psychology at Ripon College—a private liberal arts and sciences school that encourages staff to pursue further study of what makes them passionate.

Bob didn't know he was passionate about whales until, on a whim, he went whale watching with his wife, Lee, while visiting his family in Bellingham. They didn't see a whale. (No wonder he had never heard much about whales while growing up in the city.) But that led him to do additional research, which led him to discover that one of the best places to see whales was San Juan Island, a short drive and ferry ride away. He booked a trip for the next day, and this time they did see whales.

Bob could easily recall that day in 1988—"wow" was the first thing he said about it—but he still found it difficult to describe. "I'm not sure I can communicate what I felt through talking. The philosophical word *sublime* may be the closest I can get." He began to chase that feeling. Choices he made about his future seemed to relate back to that experience.

When granted an opportunity to take a sabbatical two years later, Bob chose to study orcas on San Juan Island. The Whale Museum offered him the use of Lime Kiln Point State Park's lighthouse as his laboratory, although he didn't know quite what to study at first. "I figured I would observe the effects of boats on killer whales. I had a plan to use experimental boats, moving in directions to and away from the whales. I was going to measure what happened to the whales." Bob chuckled in spite of himself. "It was really pretty silly. I hope nobody finds that original write-up."

With research from biologists such as Jane Goodall as his guide, he transitioned to simply observing the whales that passed by from shore. He and his team record how many whales swim by, which whales (when possible, they photo ID each whale by their saddle patch and dorsal fin), what vocalizations are heard on the hydrophone, and any other characteristic of noticeable behavior.

To a nonscientist, such observations may sound somewhat dry. The longer Bob engages in the research and the older he gets, the more cynical he has become himself. It's obvious the data can reveal certain trends and shifts—such as when, how often, and perhaps even why the orcas frequent the area. They may be able to determine, for example, if the area is producing an abundant supply of food or not. But what about experiences that can't be recorded?

"I was just a scientist when I came here," Bob shared. "It's not that I've ceased being a scientist. I still have the belief that science can answer a great deal of questions. But as the years go on, I just don't think that science as we know it today can answer questions like 'Why are people so passionate about these whales?'"

That particular question is one that has plagued Bob in recent years. Perhaps it's why he keeps coming back to Lime Kiln. "I never for a bit imagined I'd come back after that first year," he shared. His wife joined him the first year, but when Bob felt called to return to the island the following summer, she stayed behind to take care of the farm. He had to go, though. It just felt right.

If the answer to his burning question can't be articulated, at least it can be observed. "It doesn't matter whether you're rich or poor or what your political background is," Bob explained. "When you're out here on the rocks and the whales go by, everyone expresses themselves in the same way. I've seen really academic people just go bonkers up here." He laughed before recalling another memory.

"One time a bunch of motorcyclists pulled in with their rumble and roar. Ten or twelve tough guys with their big leather jackets came down when the whales were going by, and they acted the same as a bunch of fifth graders, jumping up and down. It was fun to see." Reactions such as these have led Bob to calling whales "the great equalizers"—everyone is equal in the face of these whales.

An interesting paradox, however, is that those with even a minor degree of whale knowledge feel compelled to verbalize it. "People say things all the time they wouldn't have said otherwise," Bob continued. "They'll say, 'Look at that whale over there; it's breaching!' without even knowing what breaching is. The whale may have simply surfaced. And that's OK; they're trying to grab the vocabulary to express what they're feeling."

Even when terms are used "correctly," Bob has a hard time accepting people's need to use them. "For so many people, particularly scientists, the use of categories such as 'breach' or 'spyhop' makes them feel good. As if somehow they understand the whales since they can label what they do." He doesn't feel those labels are necessarily appropriate from a scientific point of view, but he has learned over the years to let people have their experience. "I'm certainly not going to correct or challenge them. For them, it means a lot."

He's also not going to stop people when they come in and "*have to tell me about the last time they saw a whale.*" Bob laughed at the drive people feel to share their stories with him, but not mockingly. "If we could only harvest that enthusiasm," he pondered. Or perhaps channel it into what he has become more and more enamored with: the arts.

"The older I've gotten, the less I see science as being the only hope for these whales. I think there are other channels that we could employ that get the message out—like poetry, music." Bob paused before admitting, "Here's where I'm limited. I don't know where the arts go."

He knows art when he sees it, however. He has taken up recording some of his students reading poetry they've written about their experiences with the whales. He has marveled at children's books such as *Davy's Dream*, by Paul Owen Lewis, which tells the story of a boy's dream about wild orcas. "It just touched my heart," he shared. "The imagination that a young person has— whether they're little kids or big kids like ourselves—could generate questions that a scientist could learn from."

Bob gives himself very little credit. He insists that he lacks the gene necessary to create art or poetry himself, but even with the innate limitations of verbal language, he can give a talk that makes an audience feel something extraordinary. He speaks from so deep within his soul that a listener can't help but be moved and inspired.

The fact that so many of his interns—who at first may have arrived with only a casual interest in whales—have gone on to become dedicated whale advocates is something Bob attributes to the whales themselves. But he no doubt played a part. "I see my interns change as they work with me over a period of time. They come to articulate their feelings much better about who they are and what they want for these whales in the years to come." He added, "Being here with these whales stays with my interns for probably the rest of their lives. And that makes me feel really good." He smiled humbly.

It's not just his interns who carry their experience at Lime Kiln with them forever. Bob has countless stories of people who, like himself, have returned year after year based solely on how the whales make them feel. One story is about a young man from France who had seen killer whales on TV swimming by a lighthouse; the image ignited a passion within him to see the whales for himself.

All the man knew was that the lighthouse was near British Columbia. He put together what little money he had, flew to the northern end of Vancouver Island, and hitchhiked his way down to Victoria. While out on a boat that departed from that city, he finally spotted the lighthouse—of course, it was Lime Kiln. "I bet he was here four or five summers in a row. He camped on the island," Bob said, "and sat out here on the rocks every day, waiting for the killer whales to come by."

Another story Bob shared was of a woman from Texas who had never seen a whale, but she often dreamed about them. Her dreams led her to Lime Kiln, where she saw whales for the first time. The experience was so powerful that the first thing she did was go to the real estate office and see if she could buy a house on the island. She could—and she did.

"There are dozens of stories like that." Bob shook his head incredulously. "People who are willing to give up life as they've known it in the past, so they can be close to the whales. I just marvel at people like that; they have an incredible vision, and when it gets satisfied by seeing the whales, it formulates a plan for the rest of their lives." He shared that many people choose to get married at Lime Kiln, or some make the trip in order to propose.

As a psychologist, that phenomenon is one he wishes he understood better. "People spend thousands of dollars to come here for one reason, and that's to sit here and watch the whales. They sense that there's a benefit to that which makes it well worth the money spent. What is that benefit? I wish I knew those people better to understand what their emotional guidelines are."

Perhaps he need look no further than his own emotional guideline. What keeps him coming back? "I really want to help these whales, and this is the only way I personally know how to do it," he reflected. "One way to help them is to understand them, even though I realize that in my life time I can't possibly analyze all of this data." For that reason, Bob makes all of the data he collects freely available to anyone who is serious about studying it. He is hoping someone will look at it through the creative lens of an artist and ask the questions that, as a scientist, he never thought to ask.

"I'll do the mundane things like count the breaches and spyhops and run the analysis to see how they're correlated, but really I don't think I'm going to get very far with that kind of approach." That realization does not constitute a strong enough pull, however, for him to stop doing the research; it is only one of many variables on a long list of reasons why he should *not* come back, "I can articulate those reasons very well. My wife has to do all of the work back on our farm. I could be back at home in a recliner reading a good book," he began. "But then I find myself back here. What drive won out?"

It's possible that his drive to return isn't about the research at all, even if it was at the beginning. Maybe it's more about mentoring and educating others about this species he has come to love. Again, Bob makes decisions based on how he feels not on what he thinks. He encourages his students to do the same. "I try to inspire young people by telling them to follow their dreams. Also, I tell them that they have to create their own niche in life—it's not going to be waiting for them." These days, he feels particularly passionate about inspiring people to carve niches in the arts.

"It's very important to understand that you don't have to be a marine biologist in order to help these whales. A musician or a poet can certainly tell the story of these whales better than a scientist can." He was not saying it's easy to do, however. "It's scary, because if you're an artist, you have to 'step outside the box' in order to make money doing what you love. But I think there's room for all these different creative endeavors if you are willing to push for it somehow."

Bob believes now is the time to push for the protection of these whales. He is aware of the accumulation of threats the Southern Resident killer whales, in particular, are facing—and that those threats are the result of "a process that's been going on for many years that we didn't do anything about." He cited how oceans are getting warmer, and overfishing has been a problem for decades. "What bothers me is that the same culture that failed to respond fifty years ago still exists today."

But it won't continue to exist, if more people like him pass on their wisdom. Not everyone who comes to Lime Kiln does so with a mind and heart toward activism, but Bob does what he can to instill awareness and curiosity for the bigger picture. "I hope that we can make small changes in my lifetime in such a way that we can inspire the next generation to continue with that effort. That's my best hope." It's not too late for his generation to play a part either, he clarified. "Life is an exploration. After seventy-some years, I feel like I'm just getting started."

Learn more about Lime Kiln Point State Park at
www.parks.state.wa.us/540/Lime-Kiln-Point. Photo by Kiliii Yüyan.

JENNY ATKINSON: *Education for the Next Generation*

Jenny Atkinson's expression may appear to be deadpan, but there's an underlying sense of humor. As the executive director of the Whale Museum in Friday Harbor, Washington, her lighthearted spirit must regularly come in handy. At a small nonprofit organization, one is required to wear many demanding hats.

The museum isn't just a museum—the entity manages the Whale Hotline, Marine Mammal Stranding Network, Soundwatch Boater Education Program, two marine naturalist training programs per year, and a wide variety of educational programs. The island is a hotbed for tourism; the small community attracts hundreds of thousands of visitors per year from every state, nearly every province in Canada, and every continent except Antarctica. About thirty-five thousand of those visitors stop by the Whale Museum.

The museum's team is ready for them. As stewards of one of the only places on the island open seven days per week year-round, Jenny and her colleagues are eager to share their knowledge of cetaceans and the Salish Sea ecosystem. It's her passion—and presumably one of her life's purposes—to educate others about the environmental impacts we each make on the planet. Her gift is being able to do so in a way that is not condescending or shaming, but instead encouraging—and perhaps a bit playful.

When Jenny was eleven years old, her father gave her an SLR camera. The camera became a mechanism with which to nurture her early fascination with nature. Microscapes were her first area of interest. The fine details of plants and birds intrigued her long before the largest animals on earth completely bewitched her. She still has that camera.

Jenny's youth was split between inland and coastal states—she spent summers in Texas and was schooled in Florida. Most of the year was spent near the Intracoastal Waterway on Florida's eastern coast. She was accustomed to seeing manatees and dolphins and sea turtles in the wild, but she was also uniquely positioned to experience the early evolution of the captive industry. SeaWorld opened in Orlando just a few years after she moved to Florida as a child.

Jenny's family had already been among the first to visit Disney World, which opened a couple of years before SeaWorld. Because Jenny was a child who loved nature, SeaWorld was of more interest to her than what she called its "plastic" counterpart. It wasn't until she entered her adult years that she realized that SeaWorld wasn't really "natural." As a child, she didn't know orcas could even be seen in the wild. "I thought they were animals man had created for a theme park," she recalled.

The year 1995 changed everything. As a nonprofit professional, she had the opportunity to visit the Salish Sea for a conference, where she was told she could see orcas in the wild. Having seen orcas only in such an artificial environment, she reacted in disbelief. "If you've never experienced large wildlife, you just can't imagine that such animals could exist. I had to see them." Although she lived in a coastal state, she had never been exposed to any species of large whales in the wild. Most whale populations on the Atlantic coast have gone extinct. An estimated 250 to 500 North Atlantic Right whales still exist, although, especially in those years, sightings are rare.

Jenny came to San Juan Island and embarked on a whale watching tour. Despite heavy fog, she had the thrill of seeing a pod of resident orcas off in the distance. "It was then that it really struck me that this was just *part* of their home range. Holy moly. They're living in basically bath tubs in theme parks?! After that, I was never able to go back to a marine park or SeaWorld again. I understood captivity was not OK."

Even before she had that experience, her career had been on an environmental track. She'd started a nonprofit organization in 1985 that she'd been running ever since. The organization developed community leaders, some of whom focused on making "man-made nature more inclusive of the nature that actually belongs there." For example, one community leader worked with the military to change out the base's coastal streetlights from bright white to dim yellow, and this helped save sea turtle lives. Vehicles running over sea turtles is common in Florida. Since the creatures are genetically coded to follow the bright light of the full moon, they are drawn to bright streetlights and walk into the streets; the turtles are not attracted to dim yellow lights.

The experience on San Juan Island was more than a nudge that other experiences had offered. Jenny recalled, "When I saw the whales that first time in 1995, my whole being settled down, and I heard a voice inside my head say, 'You're home.' And that was the weirdest thing I'd ever heard, because as a child of divorce, I had moved from place to place and never felt at home anywhere. I knew at that point that eventually I would move here."

First, she finished a master's degree program at Vanderbilt University in Nashville, Tennessee, which she earned in conjunction with nonprofit work experience at the First Amendment Center. Every opportunity she had, she vacationed in the San Juan Islands— which ended up being two to six times per year for the next twelve years.

When a position opened at the Whale Museum in 2006, Jenny considered that perhaps it was time to officially make the move. Even though she'd been living in the South, her frequent trips and personal interest in whales had led her to become quite knowledgeable about the Salish Sea and Southern Resident killer whales. She had studied orca ID charts to get to know the whales individually. She had adopted multiple whales through the museum's orca adoption program.

And she had an abundance of non-whale experience that would come in handy. "I had a mentor who encouraged me to be a generalist," she explained. "He advised me to get experience in a lot of different areas so that I could fit into any niche. And that's pretty much the definition of a nonprofit director; you have to be able to fix the toilet and write a million-dollar grant."

She continued, "Every skill set you've ever developed, nonprofits will use them. It never occurred to me that I could find a job working for marine mammals without having a marine biology degree. It didn't occur to me that my ability to manage an organization and do some level of fund-raising would be just what was needed to get hired as the director of the Whale Museum."

Her experience at the First Amendment Center in Nashville would also serve her in her newly acquired role. The former was an organization that "gave a voice to the voiceless"—which is how she sees her role at the museum. "When it comes to policy and regulation, the whales have no voice," she said. "The museum's job is to speak up for them. Even though what we say might be unpopular in a larger community, if it's something that's really going to benefit the recovery of the ecosystem and the whales, then it's our job to say it."

An example of a potentially contentious community role the museum holds is its Soundwatch Boater Education Program. The program was created in 1993 as a means to educate recreational boaters on the least intrusive ways to watch whales in the wild. Volunteers are out on the water every day during the summer. If they see potentially harmful vessel activity, they courteously approach boaters and explain better practices, which are created in conjunction with US and Canadian federal governments and the international Pacific Whale Watch Association.

That's just one of the many roles the Whale Museum fulfills. Education is at the heart of every program it initiates. The museum caters to schools, camps, service organizations, and travel groups that want to receive a personal introduction to the whales of the Pacific Northwest via guided tours and presentations. Jenny recognizes that education is a critical component in the evolution of human mindset—and how environmental decisions will be made in the future.

For example, she explained how the eight- or nine-year-old kids who go through the museum are just starting to think about career choices. If they begin that exploration with an awareness of orca stewardship and their connection to the ecosystem, they are more likely to make decisions that consider impacts to the environment. Those children might grow up to be empowered to take on institutions that negatively impact the environment. "As slow as education can be, it's critical," Jenny explained. "We're trying to move masses, which requires making changes for the long-term and not just for immediate gratification."

Aside from visitor tours, the Whale Museum reaches students in all corners of the world through their Orca Adoption program. The organization sends interested teachers a packet of educational materials as part of an orca curriculum. "We have classrooms from all over the country who adopt orcas," Jenny shared. "Probably 75 percent of our members are outside of the Pacific Northwest." Inland states like Texas and Wisconsin and Tennessee represent the bulk of the museum's orca adopters.

It may seem that Pacific Northwest coastal residents would have more awareness of the issues facing the endangered Southern Resident killer whales, and to some extent that's true. But outside of niche organizations and communities, a significant percentage of the coastal population has no connection to what is happening to their own ecosystem.

Even for those who identify as orca enthusiasts, a gap often exists in their level of understanding. "I can start talking ecotypes with them and lose them," Jenny said. "I explain that these whales consist of a small family group that is on the brink of extinction, and people will ask, 'Why don't they just mate with the other whales?' or 'Why don't they just change their diets?' Those questions reveal that we have to dive deeper—if they don't understand the prey issue and how specialists are different than generalists, then they're not connecting to the ecosystem."

That lack of awareness indicates that, although they might love seeing whales, people are likely not thinking about them when they are out to eat at a restaurant and ordering a drink with a straw in it. "At what level are we connecting?" Jenny questioned. "What changes have we made due to our love of whales? Who have we told the story to? It's interesting to have that conversation with people that you think would be very connected to the ecosystem by virtue of where they live or what they love, only to discover that it might be peripheral."

Although San Juan Island attracts hundreds of thousands of visitors per year (largely due to its whale watching reputation), there has been no quantifiable study to indicate the degree to which seeing whales in the wild—which many consider a life-changing experience—actually changes behavior. "Do they just go home and show these cool photos and go back to living exactly the way they were living before vacation? Or do they start thinking about their footprint and changing what they eat and how many chemicals they're using? Nobody knows that answer."

Jenny's observations are not meant to sound overly critical. She admits that even for her, old habits die hard. "Every day I notice something I could be doing differently. Our brain is on autopilot making decisions that we don't question once we have our routine."

For those open to making changes, one of the first habits Jenny brings to people's attention is how we eat at events. While in Florida, she attended a plethora of charity banquets, and although they were in a coastal state, every one of the banquets served chicken. "Then I moved to Nashville—landlocked USA—and almost always, the dinner was salmon. Wild, sustainable, flown-in-fresh from the Copper River in Alaska. And I thought, that's not sustainable. We can't expect to live anywhere in the world and eat anything we want in any season."

Jenny began reading books like Barbara Kingsolver's *Animal, Vegetable, Miracle*, which further emphasizes the importance of eating with the seasons. It led her to change her expectations about what she thought should be on her plate. "Just because it's available at the grocery store doesn't mean it's the best quality food or the right season to consume it."

Guidelines provided by Seafood Watch and Oceanwise about safe and sustainable seafood can be helpful, but Jenny is aware of the limitations of those tools. They are based on managing harvest for human consumption. They're not factoring in ecosystem needs. "Harbor seals and orcas have just as much of a right if not more to eat salmon than I have," Jenny explained, "so rather than cull the harbor seal population, maybe we need to curb human consumption. As generalists, humans can make choices about other things to eat, whereas marine mammal diets can be very limited."

Population control is another issue that can ruffle some people's feathers, but she understands it's one that needs to be addressed. "If you look at the global scale of human activity, we're using our planet up. We need to implement political, commercial, industrial and recreational changes if we really care about the diversity of this planet and want to make sure there's space for nature, wildlife, and all of us. There are only so many natural resources on the planet that we see as ours to use, but not necessarily ours to steward."

With China's decision to stop purchasing US recycling, we may be forced to explore alternatives to plastics sooner than we're emotionally and habitually ready for. Having become accustomed to curbside collection of recyclable material, many people are upset to learn that many plastic products that once belonged in the bins are not being collected anymore—and even if they are, until another buyer is found, they may be sent to landfills anyway. We can no longer feel less guilty when we use single-use plastics because there is no longer even the illusion of recycling.

Will the public accept the environmental loss and continue using plastics that may not be getting recycled, or will we look for alternatives to plastics? Will communities and countries consider building local processing facilities, so we are not dependent on foreign countries for recycling? Doesn't shipping our garbage so far away negate the environmental benefit of recycling in the first place?

The impediment to the latter is that we are a species that typically adheres to the attitude "not in my backyard." When the dirty industrial process is in front of our eyes (and our noses), it becomes harder to deny that our current relationship to waste is not healthy or sustainable. Jenny pointed out, "China is no longer buying our recycling because processing it makes the toxin level in the air so high that it's poisoning their people. People complain about the air from China drifting over here and poisoning our environment, so shouldn't we be applauding their efforts to clean up the air? As a country, we need to stop blaming China for not buying our recycling and figure our problem out locally."

This story may seem to have digressed from the topic of whales, but Jenny is eager to remind people that everything is interconnected. "Our daily habits touch the whales. Almost every career can touch the whales. Everyone can be a local educator about aspects of their community that connect to the oceans. Ask questions such as 'What's my company's footprint on the planet?' or 'How can we give more to the planet so that we're not just taking?'"

Jenny suggests educating ourselves about the wildlife in our backyard. For example, what can we do to protect and provide habitat for honeybees? And instead of using chemicals, we can use natural gardening techniques to get rid of pests and weeds. "If we think about the global needs of our planet, we tend to get stunned and not do anything," Jenny said. "Instead, grab onto the part you can relate to and nurture that."

She has many ideas as to how to educate people on the oceans and whales, even if they're not in their backyard. "One of the things I've been wanting to do since I started working here is to create a virtual experience of this museum—virtual tours and downloadable programs—because this is an expensive and difficult place to get to."

The Whale Museum doesn't house live animals, but some educational institutions that do are headed toward replacing them with virtual experiences. Aquarium on the Bay at Pier 39 in San Francisco, for example, offers visitors close interaction with whales and dolphins through virtual exhibits. The Shedd Aquarium in Chicago offers similar opportunities; visitors have said they felt like they were in the water, swimming with the sharks.

However, Jenny is careful not to criticize people who continue to buy tickets to marine parks that still hold animals in captivity. "For millions of people, that's the only way right now that they can experience these orcas. The last thing I want to do as someone who is trying to draw people into nature is to criminalize them or demonize them for meeting the whales that way. They love them just as much as we love them; they just don't have the same level of understanding." She believes that the key is to engage those people in a way that gives them that understanding and supports them in further stewardship efforts.

Jenny does expect the institutions to step up their conservation and education efforts. Growing up in Florida, she had the opportunity to go behind the scenes and see some of the good work that the Hubbs-SeaWorld Research Institute was doing, but she now understands that such research comes at a cost. "All of those animals are paying the price for that research. The question for us as a society is, is it worth that cost? These whales positively change our lives, so what are we doing to positively change theirs?"

Those are questions she tries to bring home to the thousands of visitors that pass through the Whale Museum. Though changing generations of learned behavior is a difficult task to take on, she is "cautiously optimistic" that future generations will head in the right direction. During school group season in particular, she has reason to be hopeful.

"So many of the kids that come here have never been on a ferry or out on a large body of water before. They've heard about the whales at school, but to be in a place where they can actually see whales, or at least whale skeletons, it's really fun for them." When learning is made fun as a child, it often stays with them as adults. With Jenny's humor and enthusiasm as their guide, it's likely many of those children will become future stewards of the Salish Sea.

Details on the Whale Museum's numerous programs, along with downloadable resources for educators, can be found at www.whalemuseum.org.

JILL HEIN: *A Commitment to Service*

Jill Hein's name can be found in many places on Whidbey Island, Washington, such as on a banner hanging from a streetlight in downtown Langley and on a calendar sold at the Langley Whale Center. She has captured images of orcas and other cetaceans that have been featured in *Whidbey Life Magazine*, on the local news station's website, and in other print and online media. "The whales made me a photographer," she said. But she doesn't consider herself an "artist."

It's clear, however, that she has a keen eye and a quick reflex. She has honed her skills while serving as a naturalist aboard Mystic Sea Charters whale watching boats for the last eleven years. After retiring from an administrator position at Microsoft, Jill moved to Whidbey Island in 2004 and dedicated herself to service.

She is a board member for Orca Network, an Island County Sound Water Steward (an education, outreach, and citizen science program), a COASST volunteer (a citizen science project housed at the University of Washington which trains coastal residents to monitor local beaches), a Central Puget Sound Marine Mammal Stranding Network volunteer, and more.

Though she was born in Australia, Jill's passion for marine life didn't develop until she moved to Whidbey Island after retirement. She "hadn't even thought about whales" before moving to Washington in 1978. Jill was vacationing with her family near Kalaloch on the Olympic Peninsula when a pod of orcas swam near shore. Jill has a habit of being in the right place at the right time, without even trying.

"Another time I was out on the water when a superpod happened to be there! I saw the greeting ceremony that they do, where they all line up facing each other. I thought, 'What are they doing? Why are they hanging out like that?'" Jill was describing a ritual when extended families, or pods, of orcas reunite after time apart and celebrate being together.

Superpods occur when there is an abundance of food that supports lots of whales being in the same place at the same time. After lining up and taking an inventory of recent births and deaths in the families, the whales introduce themselves to new members before joyously leaping out of the water, spyhopping, and vocalizing rapturously. The experience is reminiscent of human families coming together for the holidays to join in a great feast.

Only the luckiest of humans get to witness this spectacle of nature. "I didn't appreciate it as I should have at the time," Jill commented. "It's something that we don't see much anymore because the pods are so broken up due to not having enough food." When Jill moved from Sammamish, Washington, to Whidbey Island, that memory of the orcas sparked her interest in becoming involved with Orca Network, which is based on the island.

Jill developed a wealth of knowledge about wildlife of the area by attending Orca Network workshops and talks, such as the Ways of the Whales workshop each January and the Welcome the Whales festival in April in honor of the migratory return of the gray whales. She additionally has taken advantage of educational opportunities through the Seattle chapter of the American Cetacean Society.

Now a certified naturalist, Jill volunteers on Mystic Sea Charters whale watching boats out of Anacortes, Washington, in the summer (orca viewing season) and out of Langley, Washington, in the spring (gray whale viewing season). Anywhere from forty to sixty passengers aboard each ride are treated to Jill's narrative about which whales are seen in the area, their habits, their diets, their migration, and the threats facing them.

She described the typical reaction of her passengers: "When they first see a whale—usually a dorsal fin rising out of the water half a mile away—they go 'Ahhhh, ohhh!' And then when we get closer, perhaps a couple hundred yards away, I don't really hear a lot out of them. I think they're absorbing the experience." Jill believes in nurturing that state of awe.

"Some of the boats out here have naturalists who talk all the time. We don't do that. When we're around the whales, we're totally quiet. I can spot who the whales are, and I'll say who it is, but that's about all until after we leave the whales." While her passengers are enjoying the thrill of what is often their first encounter, Jill takes pictures. She later posts her photos on the Mystic Sea Charters Facebook page, so passengers and non-passengers alike can have a deeper level of awareness of who was out on the water that day.

Despite having been a naturalist for eleven years, Jill's excitement for each encounter has not waned. She especially loves it when the whales swim under the boat (on their own accord—whale watching companies are under strict regulations that keep them from approaching within two hundred yards of the whales). "It's really cool when they go under the boat, and you never know where they're going to come back up. I get really excited." Her face lit up. "So excited I can't even get pictures." She laughed. "That's powerful."

When Jill can harness her enthusiasm enough to take pictures, sometimes she makes some important discoveries. The sex of a newborn orca baby was unknown until Jill snapped a picture of the calf's underside—it was a girl!

We may still be only primitively getting to "know" these whales, but to each other, no whale is a stranger. "It's mind-boggling to me that every one of those whales knows each other." Jill described the members of the Southern Resident orca population. "Each pod travels together and intermingles with other pods." Transient orcas are not members of the Southern Resident orca family, but they too have their own strong family units. "They come in their small groups, but they're always with their mother. Mom is still the boss."

Jill shared that, although Southern Resident orca superpods are becoming increasingly rare, she has seen an increase in Transient superpods in the area. "This year they've been seen more than ever before. There may be only fifteen to twenty orcas in the group, but that's a lot for Transients." Jill is partial to the Resident orcas, whose families she is more familiar with, but she never tires of seeing Transients either. "They're exciting too. It's tough to watch them eating a seal, but that's life. At least they're finding a lot of food. The Residents are hurting."

Although orcas may be her specialty, Jill has learned a lot about the area's gray whales as well. Cascadia Research, based in Olympia, consists of a team of researchers who are experts at cataloging the gray whales of the region. Whereas orcas are typically identified by saddle patches, gray whales are identified by white pigment depletion markings under their tails caused by barnacles, along with other characteristics such as rakes from orca attacks or sometimes even harpoon wounds.

Like the gray whales of Depoe Bay, Oregon, those off Washington's coast are few but consistent, stopping during their migration to feed for a couple of months. "I doubt very much that they go all the way to Alaska." Jill speculated on their migration route. "I would guess they go up the west side of Vancouver Island."

Jill is also becoming more familiar with the whales of her home country, which she still visits. "I've got a lot of places to see whales now." She grinned. "I was at my nephew's wedding a few years ago, and we saw humpbacks along the east coast. Then we went to the southern part of the country and saw the Southern Right whales. It was incredible."

When Jill is not out whale watching, she can often be found volunteering at the Langley Whale Center. Opened in 2012, the whale center gives Orca Network a physical presence on Whidbey Island. Educational exhibits detail facts and tales about the Southern Resident and Transient orca populations of the area and the North Puget Sound gray whales. Whale, sea lion, and elephant seal skulls are on display, along with gray whale baleen, bones, barnacles, and whale lice.

Another unique feature of the whale center is a lending library. Visitors are allowed to check out books, DVDs, and field guides. A small gift shop completes the center, selling everything from locally made art to jewelry and clothing with whale motifs.

As a volunteer, Jill works the cash register and answers whale questions. A map at the entrance marks recent whale sightings, as well as shore-based whale watching locations. Orca "family tree charts" are on display and for sale. "The Center for Whale Research puts out books each year with the family clans—who belongs to who, how they travel, if they split and how they're likely to be split," Jill shared. "It's really helpful."

Speaking of being helpful, Jill doesn't only staff the center, she continuously explores ways to raise money to help make the Langley Whale Center sustainable. Every year, she creates a calendar that features some of her whale photography and offers the proceeds as a donation to the center. She came up with an additional creative idea: "I painted a rock." She let out a childlike giggle. "I got a magic marker and drew a whale on the rock, and I thought, 'Hey, that's not bad looking.'" Jill started selling the rocks at the center, also for a donation.

Any opportunity she can—whether it's while volunteering at the whale center or on a tour boat as a naturalist—she aims to inspire and educate others. "I hope other people become addicted to whales too," she stated. "That's the whole goal of being a naturalist. You want people to be interested in them and care for them."

One way of caring for the whales is to care for the Puget Sound waters. "I always like to tell people on my boats, 'Yes, it looks beautiful out there, but there are problems. That water is dirty water; it's polluted and full of toxins.'" Jill has found that people from overseas are often more knowledgeable about the whales and water pollution than people from the USA.

One way many Americans demonstrate a lack of awareness (or perhaps interest) in some of the challenges the area faces is maintaining the expectation that salmon be available as a year-round, reasonably priced food. Dinner menus across the country list "Atlantic salmon" or "wild Alaskan salmon." Often, the waiters or even chefs themselves don't know how to distinguish between the two—so why would the average diner know the difference?

True Atlantic salmon are practically extinct. The ones showing up on the dinner menu are a hybrid, most likely farmed off the West Coast (fed diets of fish meal and antibiotics and food dye and bearing parasites, diseases, and deformities). Does that sound appetizing?

Not to Jill. She has completely given up salmon. She understands that even wild salmon—from Alaska or otherwise—are endangered, contributing to the lack of food for the Southern Resident orcas, who are also endangered. No longer eating fish is one lifestyle change that evolved from her activism. Though she considers herself a lifelong environmentalist, she still pays attention to other daily habits and encourages others to do the same.

"I do a presentation each year for Sound Water Stewards on cutting back or eliminating single- use bottles. We don't need them." Jill carries a reusable bottle with her. "I'm quite aware of the mess that we've created," she said. "It's really sad out there. There's so much plastic in the ocean; it's scary. And it's getting worse too."

Jill knows that the more people learn about whales and the oceans, the better nature will fare. After having lived on the island and served as a naturalist, she said, "I am more appreciative of what we have around us and what we need to do to preserve it." She encourages people who learn and care about these issues to share that knowledge with friends.

"Show them how fragile everything is," Jill began. "Teach others that if they pick up a rock on the beach, they should put it back in the same way. That's somebody's home underneath there!" That goes for the popular trend of rock stacking, as well. Although the practice of building elaborate cairns may appear to be harmless, it is potentially damaging to everything from aquatic plants to microorganisms that are attached to the rocks. Crevices in the rocks may even hold salmon eggs, waiting to be fertilized and grow into fry (larvae) that will feed off those microorganisms. For Southern Resident killer whales in particular, those eggs are critical.

Jill lowered her voice in reverence for the whales. "It's a humbling experience, a real privilege, to be able to see these whales. We're the only ones that are going to save them. We, the old ones, are the ones that made the mess. We have to do what we can to help clean it up."

Learn more about Orca Network, the Langley Whale Center, and the Central Puget Sound Marine Mammal Stranding Network at www.orcanetwork.org. *Learn more about Sound Water Stewards at* www.soundwaterstewards.org. Photo by Rachel Hein.

SUSAN BERTA: *Creating Community*

Growing up in Rock Springs, Wyoming, Susan Berta never imagined she'd live on an island. Her college course of study was music therapy, and it led her from an inland state to coastal ones: she attended Willamette University in Salem, Oregon, and then Evergreen State College in Olympia, Washington. While visiting family friends on Whidbey Island, she fell in love—first with the island, later with a man.

Her union with Howard Garrett developed out of their shared passion for whales. On behalf of Island County Beach Watchers (now Sound Water Stewards), she invited him to speak at one of the organization's retreats after learning about his campaign to release Lolita, the sole surviving orca from the Penn Cove capture in 1970, held in captivity by Miami Seaquarium. The two would go on to form not just a life partnership but a business partnership— they cofounded the nonprofit organization Orca Network together in 2001.

Susan serves as executive director for Orca Network, which is dedicated to raising awareness about the whales of the Pacific Northwest and the importance of providing them healthy and safe habitats. The organization hosts annual educational workshops, events, and a trip to the gray whale birthing lagoons in Mexico; maintains an active sightings network; operates the Langley Whale Center and the Central Puget Sound Marine Mammal Stranding Network; and still campaigns for the release of Lolita (also known as Tokitae).

Susan was a "water baby." Wyoming may not have bordered an ocean, but where there was a lake or a river, there was fascination from Susan. Her love for nature expanded the farther west she went. She joked about how when she first came to

Eastern Oregon, she was amazed at how green it was—in the desert. By the time she reached the coast, she was in awe.

After graduating from Evergreen State College and moving to Whidbey Island, she began working at an assisted living facility. At the same time, she was volunteering for Master Gardeners, an extension of Washington State University that provides public education in gardening and environmental stewardship. Through the position, she gained experience in how to run a volunteer program and developed fervor for environmental issues.

By being in the right place at the right time, she was offered a job as program coordinator for Island County Beach Watchers—an occupation she held from the organization's inception in 1989 until 2000. Thus began her love affair with whales. Previously, Susan would go whale watching in the San Juan Islands and even in Alaska—not knowing that the Southern Resident orcas came down to Whidbey Island in the fall and winter. When Beach Watchers moved their offices to the Admiralty Head Lighthouse on the west side of the island, she was in for a surprise, and a bit of pandemonium.

"I would call the Center for Whale Research [on San Juan Island] and say, 'Hey, the whales are down here!' and they'd put me in touch with people in Seattle who were interested, and then I'd call a few volunteers who were really interested in orcas and let them know the orcas were coming their way," Susan explained. She didn't know she was planting the seeds for what would become an international network of communication among whale enthusiasts.

With the advent of the internet and email came an ever-expanding list of people with whom to share whale sighting news. Susan detailed the trajectory: "My list of people to call kept getting longer and longer, so instead, I'd send out an email saying the whales were headed this way or that way, so people could watch them from shore. That turned into our Sighting Network, which turned into Orca Network and then the Langley Whale Center."

At the time, she wasn't even aware that other hotlines existed for marine mammal sightings. Cascadia Research and the Whale Museum on San Juan Island were already fielding sighting reports.

At first, those organizations feared that Orca Network's sighting reports would dilute their research and reports, but in the end, they embraced the new initiative. So many reports were brought in via Orca Network that Cascadia Research had to recalibrate some of their gray whale charts—the new numbers couldn't be compared to earlier years since they would imply there were a lot more whales, when in fact they just had better data-collecting capabilities.

What set Orca Network apart was that they weren't simply fielding calls, they were further engaging their community by sending out reports—and later building a significant online community via social media. Part of Orca Network's growth has to do with widening attention for the plight of Lolita. Susan, along with Orca Network, is still actively involved in the campaign for her release—as are people from all backgrounds, ages, and political affiliations. She shared, "We've had events where there were very conservative Republican elected officials and also some New Age people who were singing and drumming and smudging. Who would have thought that these two groups of people would be in the same room? It was Lolita that brought them together."

Shore-based whale watching has had a similar effect on people; the awe and excitement that ensues from seeing a whale in the wild is an experience that knows no political, gender, or generational boundary. Susan attested, "You never know who you're going to be watching with—it might be somebody who lives nearby or a visitor who happens to be walking by." When curious passersby inquire as to what she's looking at, Susan hands them an Orca Network card. More times than not, they end up "getting hooked" and joining the sighting network.

Susan uses each encounter as an opportunity to educate—to inform those stopping by that these whales are their neighbors and that what people do to the land and water affects these neighbors. However, she also realizes that coming together in such a way satisfies the human need for connection and being closer to nature. Though she sometimes has to share negative news about threats the animals face, she wants to turn each encounter with marine mammals and with humans into an overall positive and memorable experience.

Susan doesn't limit her outreach to adults; she recognizes that the future stewards of our oceans are our children. She shared, "It's amazing—the three- or four-year-olds we get [at the Langley Whale Center] know so much!" Even children from inland states demonstrate more awareness for the whales than ever before. "I had an order come in from Iowa for a whale CD, beanie hat, and a Langley Whale Center T-shirt. The lady said they were for her 'six-year-old orca lover.' I threw in some extra items because we love our young orca lovers!"

She may never know how far her efforts reach. Orca Network's campaign to release Lolita, for example, attracted a twelve-year-old girl from Miami who ended up becoming a model; she spoke about the captive whale in magazine articles and helped raise money for the campaign. "She still remains dedicated to her," Susan commented. "And there are other young kids raising money and bringing awareness to the cause. Sometimes it's just a phase they're going through, but for a lot of them, it turns into a lifelong passion. We try to inspire and encourage that."

Susan is no stranger to the tug at one's heart that not just orcas but all cetaceans cause in humans. Her first experience seeing a whale in the wild was in Alaska. She was there for a music cruise, but she happened to see humpback whales bubble-net feeding—a unique technique where a group of whales blow bubbles in a shrinking circle to school fish. On another Alaskan cruise in a subsequent year, she saw orcas. "That really cemented my love of whales and made me want to come home and figure out how I could get more involved locally," she shared.

It wasn't just an emotional pull for Susan—it was spiritual. The night before the orca encounter, she had dreamed she would see orcas. She can think of several occasions where the orcas seemed to read her mind. "After my uncle died, I was out on a boat trip around the island. I had been working all day and needed to sit by myself for a while and think about my uncle, and that's when the whales showed up. J-pod came right over to the boat, and they looked right into my eye." She added that since then, there have been many times when the whales have shown up when someone who was really into the whales had died. "The whales have helped me through some really hard times. They touch us in a way that we can't really explain," she concluded.

Susan's involvement with the whales took a scientific turn when the body of a dead gray whale washed up on a Whidbey Island shore. She became part of the team that helped recover the whale known as Rosie, whose skeleton now hangs at the Coupeville wharf. Though she "can't stand doing necropsies on furry things," she watched Rosie's necropsy with fascination. "I couldn't believe how big their hearts and all their organs are!" The experience led Susan to initiate the founding of the Central Puget Sound Marine Mammal Stranding Network, for which she serves as a coordinator. Though she never studied biology—she was never interested in it— she grew to love learning about the field.

Susan continued, "My story demonstrates that you don't have to go to school to be a marine biologist to do this kind of work. In Wyoming, it wasn't ever even an option." Through Orca Network, she receives a lot of inquiries from young people who want to become whale trainers because that's the only profession they know and associate with whales. If the young aspirants don't wonder about joining that field, they inquire about becoming marine biologists.

"But we need educators and naturalists and writers and musicians and artists." Susan came alive with enthusiasm. "There are so many other professions that can help the whales. That's what I really enjoy, is working with so many people in different ways to spread the word. There can't be enough books or videos or documentaries or songs because they all reach different audiences." Susan concluded, "If you have a passion for something—whether it be whales or something else that hits you in life—stay open to possibilities, and opportunities will open up for you."

Visit www.orcanetwork.org *to find out more about whales of the Pacific Northwest, educational events hosted by Orca Network and the Langley Whale Center, the campaign to release Lolita from captivity, and Orca Network's five-day annual expedition to the gray whale birthing lagoons in Mexico.* Photo by Mary Jo Adams.

IV
THE THREAT OF EXTINCTION

Due to extensive hunting in the seventeenth through twentieth centuries, some whale species have gone extinct, and others have become endangered. Sadly, whaling is not solely a commercial industry of the past. Despite the 1986 International Whaling Commission (IWC) ban on commercial whaling, Japan, Iceland, and Norway have refused to end their whaling operations.

Although Japan signed the IWC moratorium on whale hunting, Tokyo exploits a loophole by saying its hunts are for "scientific research." However, meat from its hunts has shown up in sushi restaurants as far away as California. The state subsidizes the industry, and the country used nearly US$30 million of its 2011 tsunami relief funds to support whaling.

Iceland also refuses to recognize the moratorium and allows its whalers to export hunted fin whales to Japan and to hunt minke whales to service domestic demand coming mostly from tourists. Another country that receives state subsidies for its hunts is Norway, which hunts minke whales under an objection to the ban on commercial whaling.

In addition, under IWC regulations, Denmark, Greenland, Russia, the United States, and the Caribbean nation of St. Vincent and the Grenadines are permitted to conduct "aboriginal subsistence whaling." Between 1985 and 2012, over nine thousand three hundred whales were killed under this exemption. During that same period, twenty-two thousand whales were killed in IWC member countries. There are also countries that are not members of the IWC that continue to conduct whaling cultural practices.

Beluga whales, dolphins, and porpoises are not included within the IWC restrictions and these statistics, as they are classified not as whales but as "small cetaceans." Drive hunting—a method where boats drive small cetaceans together and then into a bay or onto a beach to be slaughtered or selected for sale to marine parks—is practiced in countries such as Japan, the Solomon Islands, the Faroe Islands, and Peru. These hunts are so graphically violent that in Japan, curtains are pulled across the shoreline to hide the killings from the public. Thousands of dolphins are caught in these drive hunts each year.

Drive hunting methods that employed the illegal use of seal bombs and buzzing aircrafts were used to capture orcas in Puget Sound in the 1960s and '70s. Over fifty orcas were removed from the population—some sold to aquariums and marine parks and others killed in the process. The captures had a critical impact on the Southern Resident orca population, to such an extent that does not appear to be reversible. The population was listed as endangered in 2005 under the Endangered Species Act and is considered depleted under the Marine Mammal Protection Act. In addition to the Southern Resident killer whales, there are several threatened populations of whales:

- Norway is now hunting a higher proportion of breeding minke whale females, putting the long-term survival of this species in the North Atlantic in severe danger.
- Western Pacific gray whales, found along East Asia's coasts, are the most endangered of all baleen whales; former populations on both sides of the Atlantic are long extinct.
- The Western North Atlantic Right whale population numbers around 450, and while that number may be increasing slightly, NOAA warns the population is still "nearly extinct." The eastern population of the North Atlantic Right whale is already nearly extinct.
- Humpback whales off western Mexico are threatened, and four other populations are endangered: Central America (Pacific), Cape Verde (Atlantic), Arabian Sea, and Western North Pacific.
- Although commercial whaling of the once heavily targeted sei whale has been officially halted, the species is still subject to Japanese "scientific whaling" and is currently on the endangered

species list. Illegal whale meat found in a California sushi restaurant in 2010 was genetically traced back to Japanese sei populations.

- The beluga whale depends on sea ice for its existence and is directly impacted by climate change. Alaska's Cook Inlet beluga population is down to only around 280 whales; there were about 1,300 in the late 1970s.
- There are four recognized species of river dolphins in Asia and South America, and all are among the most endangered cetaceans on earth.
- Narwhals' long tusks make them a prime target for hunters, who sell each tusk for up to US$7,000. Narwhals are expected to suffer as sea ice melts across their Arctic habitat.
- The sperm whale population was decimated by commercial whaling in the 1800s and early 1900s. It was listed as an endangered species beginning in 1970.
- Vaquitas, also known as the Gulf of California harbor porpoise, are severely threatened by commercial fishermen, who net thirty to eighty-five vaquitas as bycatch every year.

Perhaps the best antidote to further endangerment of these species is to get to know them as individuals, not simply as numbers. Since the early 1980s, every orca in the Northern Resident and Southern Resident communities has been charted; there are established family trees for each pod. That effort could be one of the biggest reasons why these populations hold such a dear place in the hearts of so many—and therefore why more outreach has been done on behalf of protecting them. It's easier to advocate for the ones we love.

Climate change is a contributing factor that may lead some species to extinction. In only the last few centuries, human actions have significantly contributed to a rapid change in climate as a result of burning fossil fuels (coal, oil, and gas) that nature knows belong buried deep in the ground. As a result, some cetacean populations may be unable to adapt quickly enough to survive.

Loss of habitat is the most critical consequence of climate change for cetaceans, as these species exist in temperature-linked ranges. Warmer ocean temperatures and melting sea ice present challenges for large whales; in particular danger are the bowhead, narwhal, and beluga whales living in the Arctic year-round. Migration patterns that have existed for millions of years—of whales and the food on which they depend—may suddenly have to change, which also affects reproductive success and, ultimately, the survival of the species.

Food source depletion happens for reasons beyond forced migration changes too. Climate change can lead to a decrease in the population of krill, which is a primary food source for many cetaceans. Small fish depend on symbiotic relationships with other organisms, such as coral. According to the documentary *Chasing Coral*, in the last thirty years, we have lost 50 percent of the world's corals due to rising water temperatures. At this rate, more than 90 percent of the world's corals will be dead by 2050.

It is imperative that a shift in human mindset take place in order to reverse the damage that has been so consistently and heavily forced upon the earth and all species that live upon it. That shift is not impossible—it is one that some Native communities, including the Quileute of Western Washington, have undertaken in order to preserve what was at one time an abundant population and at another time nearly extinct. Previously hunted for meat and other purposes, gray whales and other cetaceans are now revered by the tribe as worthy of the utmost respect and protection—as are the waters in which they live.

BONITA CLEVELAND: *A Shift in Perspective*

A lot has changed since Bonita Cleveland's ancestors settled on the shores of the Pacific Ocean thousands of years ago—yet some things have stayed the same. A few hundred Quileute members still live and hunt in the area, although their territory has since been reduced to about one square mile around what is now the village of La Push, Washington. Their land is so isolated, sandwiched as it is between the ocean and Olympic National Park, that it is somewhat of an anomaly among developed nations. Much of the land appears similar to how it did all of those centuries ago.

One thing that has changed, however, is the tribe's relationship to whales. Always respected and revered but once hunted for sustenance, since the latter half of the twentieth century, the gray whales that pass by their shores are now only welcomed with gratitude and joy. One way in which they are received is through honorary song and dance. Since 2008, the Welcoming of the Whales ceremony has been held every spring as the gray whales migrate north from their breeding grounds in Mexico. The event is open to the public, as are the accommodations at the tribal-run Quileute Oceanside Resort.

The role whales play in their culture is not merely seasonally apparent; the whale motif is found throughout the tribe's art, stories, songs, and regalia. Bonita and many members of her family exhibit the animal's importance to their tribe by carving its image into masks, sewing its pattern onto dance regalia, weaving its design into baskets, and so much more. For the Quileute, it's impossible to separate the whale from the nation.

"I've lived here all my life," Bonita began. "I spent many, many hours on the beach here as a young child, and the whales were always there. They were just a way of life." Though it would be easy to take their presence for granted, members of the Quileute Nation know just how remarkable it is that the gray whales return to their waters every year.

The California gray whale was nearly hunted to extinction by commercial whalers in the nineteenth century and was not removed from the endangered species list until 1994, although it is still protected. Like the Makah tribe to their north, the Quileute people were granted the right to hunt whales and seals at the same time they were granted the "right to taking fish at usual and accustomed places" in a treaty signed in 1855.

Unlike the Makah, however, the Quileute decided not to petition to resume hunting the gray whale—which the tribe had ceased doing around the midtwentieth century—after it was no longer declared endangered. The former's desire to resume hunting—and their first legal kill of a gray whale in 1999 after a more than seventy-year hiatus—has been a point of contention between members of the Makah and animal activists, and even among Makah members. Since 1999, further hunts have been suspended while legal battles and environmental impact studies ensue.

Bonita is grateful that her tribe took the position it did on whaling. "In our tradition, we only take what we need, and we no longer need whale. We have lots of relations with the Makah, and we respect their ways of life, but I'm so thankful our people let the whales live their lives." When asked how the tribe came to that decision, Bonita replied, "The old people just told us to let them be. When the old people tell you to let them be, you let them be. They told us to hold them up the way they hold us up in different aspects of our culture."

One of the ways Quileute people do that is through art. "As young girls, we learned to put the whale design on all of our outfits, our dresses and our regalia." Although her dance group hasn't performed recently due to a series of deaths in the family, Bonita belongs to a dance group that has performed for the annual Welcoming of the Whales ceremony, among other gatherings. Recently, the dancers performing at the ceremony have been solely tribal schoolchildren.

With the loss of several elders in the community and the retirement of others, the responsibility for carrying on cultural traditions lies with the community's youth. "We try to teach the children the meaning behind the songs, what they're dancing to and why and whose song it is." Bonita further explained, "We have songs that all Quileutes sing, and then every family has its own songs that belong to them. When we perform, we have to say, 'We're singing (name of song) today and this song belonged to (the family name) and we have permission to sing the song because we were gifted it in (the year).'"

Bonita remembers that when she was a child, the elders taught her and her peers never to dance without a shawl or dress or hat. "That lesson stuck out in my mind," Bonita shared. "We all have dresses and hats and purses and moccasins and mukluks in our dance group, because we learned from our elders to be proud—to dress up fancy, to dance powerfully, to sing strong." She fears that ethic is faltering with subsequent generations but remains hopeful that it might be reawakened.

When her dance group resumes performing, it is likely to inspire others in the community by example. "My brother carved the whale rattles, masks, and paddles that we danced with. My son has a whale mask he performed with." Art used for dancing tends to be carved out of cedar wood and painted in a traditional style—using only black, white, and red colors. Bonita shared that the lead dancer has a rattle that represents the "lead fin," and all of the girls wear "traditional regalia and shawls on their backs." Bonita has made about forty-five of the shawls herself. "They are usually winter projects. They take a lot of work—there's a lot of cutting and sewing."

One of the dances the group has performed is to a hunting song, based on a ritual performed when members of the tribe embarked on a traditional whale hunt. Another is about the whale and the thunderbird (a mythical bird thought to bring thunder). Bonita explained that in Quileute art and in all of their dance gear, the thunderbird is seen on top of the whale. "When we were kids, we were always told that when the wind picks up, the waves will become big, and then the thunderbird will come and try to get the whale to take the whale for food for his clan, the thunderbird clan. But the whale transforms into the wolf, so the thunderbird can never catch the whale."

Although the whale may avoid the thunderbird, it seems drawn to the song and dance. "One year, during my uncle Sonny's last whale ceremony, we were at the very end of the beach, and not only did the gray whales show up, but orcas. Everybody was in awe. When you see something like that, and they come in full force, it's incredible. That was a special day."

The uncle Sonny Bonita spoke of was Fred Woodruff Jr., who was a well-respected elder in the Quileute community before his death in 2009. The two had joined forces on multiple occasions over the years to help bring Native cultural events back to the community and reinstill a sense of pride among Native peoples. Woodruff was instrumental in transforming the tradition of canoe journeys into an annual event.

Rebirthed in 1989, tribal canoe journeys trace ancestral trading routes of Western Washington and British Columbia tribes. Canoe families travel from their home nations in ocean-going canoes, many made of cedar, en route to that year's final host destination. Depending on where the journey begins and ends, the trip can take up to a month to complete. Upon arrival, visiting canoe families ask permission to land, often in their nations' languages, after which the tribes share in song, dance, and gift-giving.

Regretfully, other visions of Woodruff's haven't yet come to fruition. "It was his dream to offer whale watching trips by canoe," Bonita shared. "And he always wanted to build a longhouse here in the grass to do presentations and have traditional salmon bakes. He wanted to bring the old ways back to life. He'd say, 'Come on— we can do it, Bina! We've got to make it happen!'" Unfortunately, with his passing, the community's enthusiasm for his vision dulled as many fell into grief.

"When he passed on, the whole village missed him and still misses him, because we can see the strength of what we have now that he helped create." Bonita described how the community will honor his life through a potlatch ceremony. "In our old beliefs, our people would hold a memorial potlatch one year after the death. In modern days, it takes much longer to organize. Potlatch means 'to give away,' because gifts are given. At one potlatch, I made about fifty dance paddles to give away, painted with whales."

During dances, dancers emulate paddling to the beat of the drum and hold the paddles up when they're getting ready to land. "When you go to another reservation and you have your paddles down, that means you come in war. If you have them up, it means you come in peace." Similarly, when a paddle is given away as a gift, it is always held up, or from near the heart. Rattles are also always held at the heart during performances, unless dancers are doing the whale dance and are using the rattle in a way that represents swimming.

In addition to rattles and paddles, whales are depicted on Quileute basketry—often along with canoes, which represent the tribe's traditional hunting method. Cedar whaling hats were double-woven with an inner band and outer canoe design; one Bonita showed was a gift from her Makah family with the design of a 250-person whaling canoe. "Whaling hats told their story," she shared. "They represent how many whalers were in their canoe and how many whales they got. As the years went by, they kept adding to their hats, so they'd get taller.

Bonita said, "I remember seeing old pictures of whalers wearing these hats. The whalers' faces were all dried out with wrinkles all over from salt water damage. You could see the sadness in their eyes; they were hungry. They needed food."

Modern challenges for the tribe have less to do with the need to hunt for food and more to do with Mother Nature—and man's impact upon it. The effects of climate change are taking a toll on the tiny reservation that averages being merely ten to fifteen feet above sea level. When debris from the 2011 earthquake and tsunami that hit Japan washed up on Quileute shores, the reality of the reservation's vulnerability hit home.

Bonita currently serves on the Northwest Indian Fisheries Commission, but she earlier served as tribal chair for the Quileute

Nation for ten nonconsecutive years, during which a critical decision was made for the future of the tribe. She was part of the team who fought to regain land that had been acquired by Olympic National Park—partly due to changes in the Quillayute River's course. In 2012, then president Obama signed a law transferring 772 acres of the park land back to the Quileute Nation, allowing for the low-lying village's school, day care center, elder center, administration offices, and several homes to be relocated to higher ground.

"The land is being cleared, and the school is going to be built first. Next, the senior center and senior housing will be moving up, and then little by little, the residents whose homes are in danger will be moved up higher," Bonita shared. "Nobody wants to move, because where they live now is all they've known. But then when they saw the tsunami devastation in Japan and realize we only have six minutes after an earthquake warning to get out of the lower village and to higher ground, they understand the power of the ocean and that we can't mess with mother nature."

Rather, we have already messed with Mother Nature, she realized. "Our waters are crying for help. My heart hurts when I hear about climate change and the waters losing oxygen. The waters from Destruction Island [off the Washington coast] to the south are slowly dying." Bonita described how runoff from farmland and urban centers carrying chemical fertilizers and other toxic materials is entering the ocean and causing hypoxia, or a deprivation of oxygen, so that marine life can no longer be sustained.

She continued, "And I really hurt when I see whales that are tangled in web or cut off by a fishing line or that are being disturbed by people getting too close to them in boats. It's nice to see people get excited about seeing them, but they should watch them from afar."

However, Bonita sees a slow but steady shift in perspective in people—one that reembodies the old Native ways. "People for the most part are starting to respect Mother Nature and what she has to give. We were told by our grandparents to take care of the water because then the water will always take care of us. 'When the tide is out, the table is set,' my grandmother used to say," referring to the abundance of seafood available at low tide.

Bonita reflected upon other lessons she learned from the elders. "What gives me hope for the future of the Quileute people is teaching the way of life that we were taught. I tell people, don't be afraid to teach your children to be proud—to dance hard, to sing hard." Like her uncle Sonny, she holds a valiant vision in mind for the future. "The hope is for our people to all come together and be united and to love each other. It's so hard in our small community, because there's so much dissention that it sometimes feels hopeless to fix it. But I think everyone is at their happiest when they get to dance and sing and drum, so we need to bring more of that back."

Respect for Mother Nature and respect for each other are at the root of the lessons Bonita learned from the elders as she grew up. But the Quileute have lost so many of their elders as of late that she shared, "There are very few elders left. The strong ones need to keep teaching the way of life that we lived."

Whether Bonita is aware of it or not, she is one of those strong ones. While serving as tribal chair, she was pivotal in securing the funds and organization needed to build the Quileute Oceanside Resort, which is critical to sustaining the tribe's economy. The resort offers thirty-three oceanfront cabins, two oceanfront motel buildings, and a campground. To facilitate a closer relationship with nature, the resort does not offer televisions or wireless internet. However, with most accommodations offering a view of the ocean, guests will hardly miss technology—whale watching provides arguably better entertainment.

Bonita agrees. "To sit in the senior center and watch them still is really enjoyable to me because I know they're here yet. The whales are so much a part of our family; they are where we get our strength and our power." She paused before reiterating, "I'm so glad our people just let them be now. We're just so happy that they keep coming through."

To learn more about the Quileute Nation and the annual Welcoming the Whales ceremony, visit www.quileutenation.org. *More information on the Quileute Oceanside Resort can be found at* www.quileuteoceanside.com.

PEGGY OKI: *Environmental Art and Activism*

Peggy Oki has packed a lot of diversity into her vibrant life. Her interests span such a wide range that, rather than choosing one educational, sport, or career path, she chose several. It's the "artist side of her" that doesn't like having to commit to a particular path. Once she fixates on a goal, however, she's a force to be reckoned with.

She's always been a bit of a rebel and revolutionary. In the 1970s, she tore down walls in the skateboarding world as the only female member of the Zephyr skateboard team (Z-Boys), famous for inventing the sliding skate moves that paved the way for a whole new surf style of skating. She continues to surf and skate to this day and in 2012 was inducted into the Skateboarding Hall of Fame. Though she is still asked to speak about that historically pivotal period, she is not as interested in calling attention to her past—unless she can incorporate a bit of her current activism.

In Southern California, a curtain of forty thousand origami whales and counting is stored gratuitously in a fire-safe shipping container. Every year, two thousand origami whales are added to reflect the most recent estimate of whales slaughtered since the International Whaling Commission's (IWC) 1986 moratorium on whaling. The curtain is kept updated, should a future exhibit call for its presence.

The idea for the Origami Whales Project developed out of Peggy's desire to visually and publicly demonstrate how many whales are still being killed. Like many members of the general public, she thought whaling became history after the moratorium. In 1999, however, she uncovered the unfortunate truth after an unusual encounter with a gray whale.

She was surfing when she said, "From fifteen meters away, a gray whale lifted its head out of the water, looked around, and met my eye." She was thrilled to have such a unique and intimate experience, but she couldn't help but wonder why it had happened. "It's very rare for a whale to come that close to a human in their own environment, so I thought I needed to look into what issues they were facing at the time."

She was horrified to discover that although commercial whaling had been banned, exceptions granted to various countries mean approximately two thousand whales are still being hunted every year. (That number is remarkably higher when it incorporates dolphins and other small cetaceans—Japanese drive hunts alone kill nearly twenty thousand dolphins, porpoises, and small whales every year.)

That news was heartbreaking for Peggy. A love for the natural world was instilled in her at a young age through *The Undersea World of Jacques Cousteau* and through surfing. She has swum with dolphins, watched whales pass near the shore, and turned her love for cetaceans into art. She began illustrating wild animals as an undergraduate biology student at the University of California, Santa Barbara. She went on to earn a bachelor of fine arts degree in painting, with an emphasis on environmental art.

Her Origami Whales Project perfectly melded her passions and skills. In the spring of 2004, she announced her goal of collecting one thousand four hundred origami whales for a large-scale public art project, and people responded so much so that the idea evolved to collect thirty thousand origami whales for a "big curtain" of whales. Thousands of children and adults from all over the world contributed origami whales for the cause. Nearly five hundred whales were made at the Santa Barbara Whale Festival, and the rest came in the mail from supporters, including young students, who'd heard of the project from the media.

"What I love about this project is reaching kids," Peggy shared. "When teachers contact me and say they'd like to get their classrooms involved, it becomes a lesson about conservation and empowerment. There's something tangible the kids can do to make a difference—they can fold whales." Peggy smiled. "I feel grateful to have the opportunity to create art that has meaning and that empowers through participation." Adult volunteers also helped hand-stitch the thousands of whales into strands. The finished product was then presented to the US IWC whaling commissioner in Washington, DC, in 2004.

The first public exhibition of the Curtain of 30,000 Origami Whales was in May 2007 in Alaska at the fifty-ninth annual IWC meeting. It was a powerful visual statement, memorial, and call to action. At a height of five feet and a length of over four hundred feet, the curtain formed a maze. IWC delegates were invited to attend a reception and walk through the curtain. The exhibit garnered media attention in Anchorage, furthering the project's outreach, and Peggy's project was invited to exhibit at the Alaska Oceans Festival that same year. The curtain has twice exhibited at the Maui Whale Festival in Hawaii, where over a thousand visitors walked through the maze each year, some being moved to tears.

Peggy's involvement in cetacean protection may have skyrocketed after her intimate encounter with a gray whale, but it was not the first time she'd studied them or undertaken activism on their behalf. She began studying cetaceans in the 1980s after seeing dolphins for the first time and being moved by how playful they were—which she knew to be a sign of intelligence. "I had long been interested in animal behavior in their natural habitat, so my experience with the dolphins led me to study marine biology and field zoology," she shared.

Sperm whales caught her attention. "I'm a sperm whale groupie." She laughed. "My personal dream is to get in the water with sperm whales. They're just so fascinating—they have the world's largest brain, they're the world's largest toothed mammal, they're highly social. They stay together with their families for a very long time.

"The biggest thing that grabbed me besides their intelligence is that even though they are the largest toothed mammals, they have made no unprovoked attacks on humans. They took such a big hit with whaling because they never abandon their injured or sick. Whalers would harpoon a smaller calf, tie it to their boat, and wait for the rest of the pod to swim over to try to save and protect it. The whalers would then wipe out the whole pod. Scientists are still not sure if the species will fully recover from whaling."

Peggy's interest in a plethora of subjects and her free spirit called her outside the classroom and into the wilds. She embarked on an array of travels, following warm climates and good surf. She surfed, she skated, she rock climbed, and she created art. She also became an activist for whales and dolphins.

She said, "That was at a time when tuna fishing operations, primarily off Central America and Mexico, were chasing dolphins into their nets. Literally tens of thousands of dolphins were drowning in these nets every year because fishermen thought that if they could chase them into the net, there would be yellowfin tuna swimming underneath them that they could catch as well." The fishermen attempted to release the dolphins after their capture, but they were seldom successful, and the stress alone caused the dolphins serious damage.

Peggy was one of the early campaigners who helped bring public awareness to this practice that, in the 1980s, resulted in the death of more than one hundred thousand dolphins annually. (An estimated 6 million dolphins have been killed since the Eastern Tropical Pacific [ETP] fishery began in the 1950s). In 1990, the US government imposed an embargo on tuna imports caught with purse seine nets in the ETP waters and enacted the Dolphin Protection Consumer Information Act. The law states that to label a product "dolphin-safe," the tuna must not have been caught in a way that chased, encircled, or killed dolphins.

Though there is still serious need for new tuna fishing regulations and sustainable practices, dolphin deaths today are estimated at a much lower one thousand per year. A more sobering statistic is the estimated three hundred thousand marine mammals that die annually from accidental capture in fishing gear, making bycatch one of the largest threats to cetacean populations and marine ecosystems around the world.

Japan is another hotbed for Peggy's whale and dolphin activism. She is Japanese American, so presenting her work there takes on deeper meaning. In 2010, during Japan's Dolphin Day, an activism event organized by Ric O'Barry (an animal trainer turned activist, famous for having captured and trained dolphins used in the TV series *Flipper*), Peggy exhibited a curtain of one thousand two hundred origami dolphins in Tokyo. It was shortly after the documentary film *The Cove* exposed Japan's dolphin drive hunting practices to people around the world. It's hard to say how significant of an effect such activism has had, but Peggy has reason to feel hopeful.

"There's definitely a group of citizen activists in Japan who have taken this issue on. They've held protest marches on Japan Dolphin Day and gone to the Taiji Whale Museum to put posters up and raise awareness about the slaughters. They probably get taken away quickly, but there are people on the ground of Japanese nationality doing something."

Back at her home base in California, she organized another endeavor to bring attention to Japan's whaling practices. After Japan announced they would be killing fifty humpback whales in Antarctica, Peggy used photo identification records of actual humpback whales sighted off Antarctica to paint a portrait series of fifty individual whales. The series was exhibited to positive response.

Another campaign Peggy has initiated is Let's Face It, which is a visual petition put in place to protect the Maui's dolphin. This subspecies of dolphin is found only off the coast of New Zealand, and it is the world's smallest and rarest marine dolphin. Due to entanglement and drowning in gill nets (a fishing net that is hung vertically so that fish get trapped in it by their gills) and recreational set nets (a fishing net fastened in fixed position), only around sixty adults are left in the wild.

To bring attention to the severity of their situation, individuals have their picture taken with a photo of the Maui's dolphin, which gets sent to the New Zealand government. "Instead of signing your name to a letter, there's a photo that shows a face," Peggy explained. People all over the world have contributed, and over nine thousand four hundred "faces that want to save the Maui's dolphin" have been presented to the government as a petition to ban gill netting in the Maui's dolphin habitat.

Peggy additionally created a curtain of origami Maui's dolphins, representing the 111 that remained in 2006, which exhibited at the Museum of New Zealand Te Papa Tongarewa for three months followed by the Waikato Museum in New Zealand for two months.

As if all of that weren't enough, this is Peggy's fifteenth year in a row volunteering at New Zealand's Maui Dolphin Day, where she annually organizes art actions. "I got kids and adults to color in a postcard I designed that has a couple of Maui's dolphins on it for them to send to friends and family across the country. There's still not enough awareness about the dolphins, so the more people that learn about them, the more there will be who hopefully ask the government to take action."

She created a video petition called Christmas for Lolita, a compilation of people around the world asking to have their Christmas wish of her release back to her pod fulfilled. Similarly, she organized a Valentines for Lolita campaign, collecting Valentine's Day cards that were sent to the owners of the Miami Seaquarium, where the killer whale has been held for nearly forty-eight years.

Peggy also leads traditional letter and signature collections. A template for a letter is on her website and can be printed and signed and sent to her—she has over two thousand and counting, which she is holding onto for an opportune moment and manner to present them to the Seaquarium.

Clearly, Peggy is persistent. There are so many causes to champion, however, that her resources often get stretched thin. Ideally, she'd love to bring the Origami Whales Project to every IWC meeting, but it has gotten so big that shipping costs have become excessive (to the tune of tens of thousands of dollars). She does accept tax-deductible donations via a fiscal sponsorship through Cetacean Society International and is hopeful she'll be able to exhibit her curtain of origami whales again.

In the meantime, she supports her activism through her art and through public speaking. The former is undertaken through the design and sale of handmade greeting cards, which are all nature-focused and most often ocean-themed and based on her paintings. The latter is her current priority. "My ultimate goal at this time is to secure more public speaking appearances where I talk about my environmental art and actions on behalf of whales and dolphins." An example of one of her talks can be seen online—she was a speaker for TEDx Queenstown in 2016.

She admits she is not a fan of fame—after the documentary *Dogtown and Z-Boys*, about the 1970s Zephyr skating team she was a member of, came out in 2001, she got another taste of it. "I'm not into that," she shared, "but what I've always appreciated about celebrity status is that when movie stars or other celebrities come out and talk about what they care about, they get people's attention. People listen." Peggy beamed her signature smile and added, "My little phrase is 'I work it for the whales.'"

For more information on Peggy's art, activism, and public speaking—and to learn how to support her campaign efforts—visit www.peggyoki.com. Photo by Matt Dayka.

HANNAH FRASER: *A Servant of the Sea*

While giving a Tedx Talk in Valencia, Spain, Hannah Fraser reminded her audience that the term *mermaid* can be broken down into *mer* ("sea") and *maid* ("servant"). Thus, to be a mermaid is to be a "servant of the sea." It is a role she has gladly assumed for herself. She has found a way to combine her passion for swimming with her commitment to ocean activism by becoming a "professional mermaid"—an underwater performance artist and model.

Today, a thriving mermaid subculture exists, but when she began her career in 2003, she was an anomaly. Not only did she have to forge her own unique career path, she had to create her own mermaid tails (that were both beautiful and functional) and overcome the stigma that comes with being the first to label herself what was understood to be a mythical creature.

Hannah believes in the possibility of transforming fantasy into reality. From her childhood dream of becoming a mermaid to her vision of swimming with tiger sharks, humpback whales, and manta rays—all in the name of art and activism—she has demonstrated to countless young girls that no dream is too big to manifest.

In addition, her work has proven that passion can lead to profound purpose; footage of her performances has been instrumental in helping to change governmental protection laws for manta rays and sharks. She is on a mission to end cetacean slaughter by showing people that "these animals are intelligent, interactive, largely harmless, and invaluable to the balance of the ecosystem that we depend upon for life." If anyone can accomplish such an enormous task, a mermaid can.

One of Hannah's earliest, and most infamous, forays into ocean activism was coorganizing a peaceful paddle-out ceremony in the literally bloody waters of the Taiji cove in Japan where thousands of dolphins and pilot whales are routinely slaughtered. Dressed as a mermaid, she was among over thirty celebrities, musicians, and activists whose presence in the waters angered fishermen to the extent that they attacked the protestors with long fishing sticks and pushed them dangerously close to boat propellers.

A number of dolphins had already been slaughtered by the time the group arrived in the waters. "We held a circle for twenty minutes while the remaining live dolphins squealed and spyhopped, looking at us and moving toward us as if they knew we were there to help," Hannah recalled. "We were unable to free any of them as the cove was roped off by fishermen. Eventually we had to leave and all of the dolphins were slaughtered."

Footage from the event made its way into the Oscar Award–winning documentary *The Cove*. The film brought global attention to the useless killing that still occurs six months out of the year in Japan. The practice is known as drive hunting, and it is legal in the country; the hunts are argued to be part of Japanese culture, although they did not begin until 1969.

Despite bringing increased awareness of the cruelty of Japan's practice of cetacean slaughter, Hannah noticed that widespread exposure to the film was unlikely to occur. There is a limit to human tolerance for tragedy. "The common response I heard when telling people about the film was 'I don't want to see dolphins being killed, but I support what you do!' It seems many of us aren't willing to face reality when it's ugly."

That was a critical realization for Hannah. She had to figure out how to engage people in the telling of tragic circumstances in a way that inspired passion and purposeful action rather than instilled guilt and trauma. She had to create imagery people would *want* to look at. It was a good thing she was already an artist and a model—and a mermaid.

Hannah was born in England (where her "hippy traveling mother" met her "rock star father of the seventies band Free") and raised in Los Angeles until the age of seven. After her parents separated, she moved with her mother and younger sister to

Melbourne, Australia, at least a two-hour drive from the beach. Her life near the ocean began after she finished school and moved to the subtropical paradise of Byron Bay on the east coast of Australia.

But as a child, she did have access to the public pool, which was a fortunate thing, since she felt most at home underwater, just like a mermaid. "As a kid," she explained, "I naturally swam with my legs together and felt totally comfortable underwater. I even drew stick figures with tails!" Becoming a professional mermaid was a natural evolution of the artistic pursuits she'd undertaken her whole life. From a young age, she would create mermaid art and sculptures that she'd decorate with shells and seaweed.

She came up with the idea to create her own mermaid tail after seeing the film *Splash* when she was nine years old. "I realized being a mermaid didn't have to be a fantasy in my head. I could actually embody it on this planet." With the help of her mother, she converted an orange plastic tablecloth and pillow stuffing into a mermaid tail. "I loved it so much that I swam around in my pool in it for months on end until it disintegrated!"

Putting on a mermaid tail and going swimming suited her childhood fantasies and her personality. She recalled having been an extremely shy child who found solace in the ability to express her passion without the use of words. "I found it challenging to put my feelings and emotions and dreams into words and share them, and when underwater, there was no pressure to communicate this way."

Her shyness may have been the result of having moved around so much as a child—she went to fourteen different schools before the age of ten. "I was always the new girl, and that either imbued me with an uncomfortable power of others interest in me or a downright ostracism, which often left me swinging on the playset alone and crying." Hannah's strength of character was apparent even then, however. "At age twelve, I realized I didn't like myself and wouldn't want to be friends with me either. I decided to do one thing every day that scared me; whether it was speaking up in class or talking to the cute boy I liked, I started taking steps to become the kind of person I could admire."

Even after she gained self-confidence by moving toward fear in such ways, she always felt more at ease using her body and her art to express herself. At twenty years of age, she began her career as a fantasy artist—an artist whose work represents mythological, magical, and supernatural themes. In addition, she was modeling, costume designing, and working as a photographer. Those various occupations would give her all of the prerequisite skills needed to later start a mermaid performance business.

The idea to forge a career as a mermaid began after she was invited to attend a casting call for an underwater modeling shoot. The experience turned her on to her natural ability to perform underwater. "At that point, all of my passions converged, and I became the living example of my artistic dreams," she shared. "I stopped working my other jobs as a photographer and an artist to become a full-time mermaid."

First, she needed to make a tail. "Now you can simply go online and purchase a tail, but at that time, there was no such thing. I had to create everything from scratch. After countless hours of trying different techniques, I had my first legit prototype mermaid tail." That was 2003. Fifteen years later, she has over fourteen fully functional tails, all handmade. Each tail takes her approximately six months to make and costs thousands of dollars to create. "There's a lot of intensive sewing, gluing, and constructing. It's a labor of love but worth it in the end. My tails are functional, durable, and very beautiful!"

She began doing underwater shoots that were motivated by her passionate dedication to ocean conservation. The images started attracting media attention. "Then people actually began to hire me as a mermaid!" she shared. "My fantasy became my reality." To her knowledge, she became the first person to make a full-time career out of being a freelance, professional mermaid.

Hannah decided to move to Los Angeles in 2010 in order to more easily access job opportunities. She has since been hired by many of the world's top aquariums (that pass her stringent animal ethics test), performed at large-scale events, and been featured in photo shoots, campaigns, and short films for many large companies and creative ventures.

The experiences that have been most dear to her heart have been filming in the ocean with no thought for profit. "Those have been the experiences that have been the most powerful and moving for me, and for the people who have seen my videos. For example, the footage of me swimming with humpback whales in Tonga ended up being shown worldwide and blowing people's minds as to what's possible in terms of connecting with underwater animals."

Those videos, inspired by creative and passion-driven purposes, are the ones that have successfully served as platforms for ocean activism. Hannah described her experience swimming with a humpback whale and her calf: "We were way out in the ocean, looking down at the endless blue depths. Suddenly, the mother began to surface underneath me, getting larger and larger. I realized I could end up in this whale's blowhole or mouth, but the whales seemed so aware of their own size. It was amazing how conscious the mother was of its effect on me, down to the swishing of its tail. You can feel that intelligence emanating from them; you look them in the eye, and there's this ancient *consciousness* looking back."

To Hannah's amazement, the whales started singing to each other. "It was mind-blowing. The mother's song was so deep and so rumbly, it was like standing in front of the largest speaker stack in the world—it was this massive whale rock concert that caused my ribs to vibrate. I felt like it was rearranging my DNA molecules; it was reverberating through every cell in my body. The baby whale was singing in such high-pitched trumpeting notes that it was nearly too loud and too high-pitched for my ears to deal with. And of course, water carries sound, so I could feel it coming from every angle. It was just phenomenal.

"When we got back in the boat, I cried; it was a powerful emotional release. I knew at that moment that I would put my life on the line to protect these creatures. I felt so grateful that even after hundreds of years of humans decimating their species, they're still so interactive, joyful, and curious."

The experience led Hannah to cocreate a short film with cinematographer Shawn Henrichs that portrayed the beauty of humpback whales and the interspecies exchange that took place. The film, *Betrayal*, ends with a twist, drawing attention to the dichotomy of the human fascination with whales and the human habit of killing anything that is larger, stronger, and not entirely understood.

She hopes that such work will eventually lead to the cessation of cetacean slaughter—just like a video the pair cocreated of swimming with manta rays (called *Manta's Last Dance*) helped convince the Convention for International Trade of Endangered Species (CITES) to list manta rays as a protected species. (Manta rays are harmless beings that are hunted relentlessly for their gills, which are sold on the Asian food market.)

Another short film Hannah cocreated showcases the community of Oslob in the Philippines, where fishermen put an end to their participation in the shark-finning trade. "They began sharing the shrimp that they caught with the whale sharks and making friends with them. A small, noninvasive ecotourism project to introduce whale sharks to visitors began. The locals realized that it is more profitable to live in harmony with the animals and to showcase their natural beauty. That venture is a great blueprint for the way we can interact with wild animals without killing or capture."

The species she feels most passionate about are whales and dolphins. Being able to swim close to humpbacks and dolphins is what inspired her to campaign against ocean degradation, pollution, and overfishing. "Being a mermaid gives me a firsthand perspective of what is going on in the ocean in different parts of the world," she shared. "I have swum in the most beautiful pristine locations and also the most polluted waters [with] rubbish-filled beaches. I have seen sick, beached animals, and I've seen coral reefs dying."

Hannah feels that, as part of the human culture responsible for that degradation, she needs to do what she can to "help with the mess we have created in our lust for commercialism and our 'throw-away' culture." Through her public speaking, she promotes sustainable lifestyles. She eats only vegan and chooses organic food wherever possible, supports ocean conservation organizations, and uses her mermaid persona "to inspire people to connect to the underwater world and care about the amazing creatures who live within it."

She understands that the sustainability of our oceans is a matter of life and death not only for the species that live within them but for us. "The ocean is our lifeblood. Under current estimates, around 70 percent of earth's oxygen is produced by the sea, and around 70 percent of all life on earth exists in our oceans. If we continue to pollute and overfish our oceans, it's only a matter of years before the rest of civilization crumbles. We can't survive without the ocean. It's the womb of the world."

What the oceans need is an upsurge in "servants of the sea." Thankfully, a mermaid industry has evolved over the past decade— significantly due to Hannah's trailblazing. The growth of people swimming as mermaids as a profession or hobby and often as a form of activism comes as no surprise to her. "I think the mermaid is a symbol of man's connection to nature in a very visual way. At this time when our oceans are so threatened by pollution, oil spikes, global warming, and trash islands, it's interesting to see the resurgence of mermaids as figureheads for standing up for ocean life."

Being a mermaid is not just a job for Hannah—it's a lifestyle. From the moment she wakes up, she strives to cultivate the level of physical fitness necessary to sustain working in challenging underwater conditions. She practices yoga and breath work and dances to maintain a flexible spine. Her daily commitment to the career has made it possible for her to hold her breath for up to two minutes while performing underwater; she can free dive fifty feet below the sea and return on one single breath.

She wears no oxygen tank, no warmsuit, and no face mask. She feels as though the tail gives her "superhuman powers" that allow her to maintain the necessary speed and maneuverability to swim with whales and dolphins. Her movement has to be fluid to be aesthetically pleasing in photos and film—her body must undulate, like a dolphin's. In addition to the intense physical hardships of her work, a deep knowledge of the ocean and its inhabitants is required—especially when swimming with apex predators of the ocean (such as tiger and great white sharks).

After successfully studying with trained professionals, Hannah developed the awareness that she can face her deepest fears. "I scared off a fourteen-foot great white shark that was coming at me, so whenever I'm faced with scary situations in life, I remember that and think, 'I can handle anything!'"

Not everyone can, or should, attempt to do what she's done. "When I am asked to refer other mermaids for events, there are only a handful that I know who are capable and professional enough to pull it off," she explained. "To be able to create convincing mermaid photos and footage, you need to have a very strong breath hold ability, [have] an extremely strong swimming ability (with your legs bound together), be able to look comfortable and beautiful underwater, be dive certified, not be afraid of underwater wildlife, have ocean experience in tides, currents, waves, varying temperatures, be able to swim with your eyes open underwater without goggles, and have modeling experience!" And if that's not enough, she added that "to appear in public, you need to be outgoing, personable, friendly, confident, and unafraid of looking like a freak!"

She doesn't want to deter anyone from pursuing their passion, however. She receives messages daily from fans around the world who feel inspired by her to pursue careers as mermaids. "We live in a time where radical creativity is needed more than ever," Hannah deeply believes. "Fantasy and imagination are the source of innovation and solution."

Her advice for everyone—not just aspiring mermaids—is to "find that place inside yourself that connects to the source of nature and the earth we live on. Then act from this place of reverence and care in all aspects of your life. Be vocal about your love of the earth and humanity. Find ways to support organizations that are doing real positive work to help bring in a new paradigm of society based on mutual respect for all creatures and humans. Use your work or art form or hobbies to bring awareness to issues that need help with positive change."

For Hannah, creating a career that fit into her passion rather than trying to fit into an existing career path was not easy—but it has been endlessly rewarding. "I fly around the world, and I get paid to perform underwater," she stated. "As soon as I owned this new profession for myself—when I claimed what I saw as my goal—the offers started pouring in. Which goes to show that if you are passionate about something, it doesn't matter how unusual it is—there is a market for it!"

Perhaps the success of her business is a direct result of having pursued a path with purpose—one that is based on the natural attractants of love and respect. "I will always stand up for what I believe in and use my creative talents to bring awareness to issues that need attention," Hannah said. "But I hope to do it in a way that will inspire change and not just point a finger and create shame."

The beautiful artistry expressed in her underwater photos and videos undeniably accomplishes that goal. By bringing fantasy and mythology to life, she reminds us of our capacity to view the world as a child does: with awe and wonder and a core belief that anything is possible—even the ability for all humans and creatures, underwater and land-based alike, to coexist peacefully as one.

To view Hannah's underwater modeling and performance art, visit www.hannahmermaid.com. Photo by Shawn Heinrichs, Blue Sphere Media.

HOWIE COOKE: *Where There's a Wall, There's a Whale*

Ask Howie Cooke about his love of the sea and you may be in for a long sail. He has initiated so many campaigns, crusades, and art projects in support of the ocean and cetaceans—"minds in the water," he calls them—that it would be impossible to describe them all briefly.

Much of Howie's activism revolves around visual media; an epiphany in the 1970s led him to take up painting large canvases to represent both the beauty of cetaceans and the threats facing them. Some of his work is captured in several documentaries with professional free surfer (meaning, noncompetitive) Dave Rastovich. The two joined forces in 2004 to found Surfers for Cetaceans (S4C), a nonprofit organization dedicated to activating surfers and the surf media—along with the public—against whaling and dolphin kills. Howie's activism extends far beyond his affiliation with just one organization, however.

Although Howie is a New Zealand citizen and Australian resident, his murals can be found all over the world, in countries such as Portugal, Morocco, Thailand, the Philippines, Fiji, Chile, Costa Rica, and the United States. His travels are often dictated by where the annual International Whaling Commission (IWC) meeting is being held or where a campaign relevant to S4C is.

Howie's big-picture vision may be a result of where he was born and raised: in the highest house in Auckland, New Zealand. From that ridge, he could see from the sweep of the country's wild, black sand beaches on the west coast to the white sand stretches of the eastern shores. The unique landscape inspired his artistic pursuits from an early age, as did his initial interaction with the sea.

"When my family moved down from the hills to near the sea, I was that kid who would explore the tidal pools in search of strange creatures." He laughed. "Soon, I started drawing the marine world and collecting fossils. I was a very curious kid with lots of microscopes." As a teenager, he became more acquainted with the ocean when he began body surfing and diving, and his fascination with the "tropical wonderland of the ocean" soared while living on a remote island west of the main island of Fiji in 1975.

The following year, while living on Waiheke Island back in New Zealand, Howie had an epiphany that changed the course of his life. "In one moment, I grasped the immensity of who whales are and understood the importance of seeing earth as Planet Ocean." In pondering whales and dolphins not only having huge brains but also having huge hearts, he felt it evident that cetaceans are highly evolved beings of great intelligence and huge compassion.

Their behaviors even seem to represent spiritual lives. "Living in a gravity-free space, they are like tai chi masters or free-wheeling dancers who gracefully offer us unconditional friendship, good humor, and forgiveness," Howie observed. He became captivated by their beauty but also highly disturbed by the degree to which they were disappearing. He was aware that they were being hunted en masse, in particular by Russia and Japan. "That's when I decided to be a voice for the whales and dolphins. It suddenly became imperative that I paint big canvases and celebrate this great nation."

Howie also became a vegetarian (eventually vegan) to "be that voice and have the best relationship I could with the animal kingdom." He completed his first large whale painting, of a humpback whale mother and calf, titled *If You Know the Reason Why*. He also worked with Project Jonah New Zealand, a charity that inspires citizens to care for and protect marine mammals and the oceans, illustrating and presenting. Playing guitar in a rock band offered his main income while he grew his painting path.

His *Reason Why* painting referenced the question he was asked repeatedly by visitors: "What are you painting whales for?" In that era, there was not much public interest in or knowledge of whales and dolphins. "It probably seems incomprehensible now," he said, "but in those days, whales and dolphins didn't have protections and were often referred to according to their different body parts or how long it took to kill them." An example of the latter are Right whales, named because they swim slowly and float after death—making them the easier and therefore the "right whales" to kill.

"They were being slammed everywhere," Howie shared. "Many species were on the verge of disappearing; it seemed the miracle of whales was passing away forever just as the new underwater photography and film era was showing the world the wonder of them and the ocean herself."

Howie's paintings weren't just beautiful depictions of the underwater world—they were often political statements about the many threats facing cetaceans and other marine life. He used art as a means to address these issues in a visual way. Sailing among the South Pacific islands brought him into contact with humpback whales who were recovering from the very edge of extinction. "I was standing on a reef on Eua watching humpback whales coupling, not long after the king of Tonga banned whaling in 1979, and was inspired to celebrate this hopeful way forward with an oil painting called, in Tongan, *Let's Love the People of the Sea*."

Tonga is a hotspot for humpback whale breeding; the whales undertake one of the longest migrations in the world when departing from their Antarctic feeding grounds to the warmer waters of the South Pacific where they court, mate, and calve. The six main populations of southern hemisphere humpback whales were decimated over time, starting with the Yankee whaling ships of the eighteenth century through to the modern era, particularly in the 1950s to 1970s, when forty-eight thousand humpbacks were taken by the then Soviet Union—twenty-five thousand of these were illegally killed from just 1959 to 1962 as they migrated past New Zealand on their way to Tonga and Fiji. The number of humpbacks in the Tonga population was estimated to have fallen from a pre-whaling peak of about ten thousand to fewer than one hundred, with possibly only fifteen of those being breeding females, by 1964.

"The hunting of traumatized orphan juveniles in the Tonga breeding grounds heavily impacted this group, and frankly, it is a miracle they have recovered, albeit in a very small way," Howie shared. "Elsewhere in the Pacific islands, there are very small remnant populations slowly recovering from a genocide that was unleashed on them along most every part of their migrations between birthing grounds in warm upper latitude waters in winter and feeding grounds in the cold southern waters during Austral summers." A thriving whale watching industry has since evolved in Tonga, contributing to the economy of the region via tourism, as the Tongan humpback population is estimated to be around two thousand in now protected exclusive economic zone (EEZ) waters, a sea zone over which a state has special rights regarding exploration and use of marine resources.

Howie's activism didn't end with art; while living in Bondi Beach, Australia, he spearheaded a movement to eliminate cigarette butts from public beaches with a small group he formed called the Grainies. Their tactics ranged from confrontational— "We would not back down against people littering the beach, and we took on every single cigarette tosser who used the beach as an ashtray"—to creative: "I made big, fake cigarettes that looked real and laid them along the beach pathways with signs that read, 'How big does your butt have to be before you see that it's litter?!'" The latter was part of a campaign Howie instigated called Get Your Butts Off Our Beaches, which evolved into a national campaign.

He even used cigarette butts in an art exhibition called Devalued Art for a Desecrated Planet in order to draw attention to the issue. "I glued cigarette butts directly onto several paintings I had done of dolphins, turtles, and cephalopods, which shocked most people. I was asking why is putting butts on paintings so shocking, given that people generally accepted smokers throwing them into the street, into storm-water drains, and into the sea. Is art really more valuable than the planet that sustains our very existence?!"

Howie fully reinvolved in anti-whaling campaigning when he began attending IWC meetings in 2000 and campaigning for additional whale sanctuaries (areas of the ocean where whaling is prohibited). He knew that the IWC had approved the Indian Ocean Whale Sanctuary in 1979, effectively shutting down the Russian hunt of sperm whales, and in 1994 had established the only other IWC-designated whale sanctuary, the Southern Ocean Whale Sanctuary near Antarctica. Now, he wanted to make a visual statement in support of the South Pacific Whale Sanctuary, a proposed region of the South Pacific Ocean in which whaling would be prohibited.

To highlight New Zealand's proposal, he once again turned to art at the year 2000's IWC meeting in Adelaide, Australia. He created for the International Fund for Animal Welfare (along with the help of over one hundred kids from nine different schools) a thirteen-by-six-meter painted banner of the islands and countries in the region and incorporated once again the Tongan words for "let's love the people of the sea."

Prior to the 2001 IWC meeting in London, he brought the banner to a meeting regarding the South Pacific Whale Sanctuary in Samoa. There, Howie got nearly all the government representatives from every South Pacific nation including Australia and New Zealand to place their hands in blue paint and "sign" the banner with their handprints.

Howie explained, "It was a very good way of using art to make a statement, because it created a document that, unlike a written document, was irrefutable. It's clear that humans are adept at writing all these caveats and excuses for themselves and changing the rules at a moment's convenience. By placing their handprint on that banner and having it on film, nobody could later say, 'Oh, we didn't really support the proposal.'"

The banner was brought to the IWC meeting in London and hung right outside the main entrance, but it was generally too cumbersome to display. Back in Australia, Howie came up with the idea of a painted tipi, which served as a 3-D banner that represented a dedicated space for the whales. "In 2002 at the IWC meeting in Japan, we took the whale tipi right into the mouth of the dragon, a whaling port in Shimonoseki, and effectively created an embassy for the whales from which various pro-whale environment ministers from around the world read their press statements to the assembled media.

"It had this natural power," Howie said. "Japanese whalers were threatening to kill me, but they wouldn't come near the whale tipi. Beautiful things happened. A Shinto priest prayed inside of it for world peace. A Japanese journalist broke down in tears. A local man, Izumi Ishii, who used to kill dolphins but who is now a major advocate for the dolphins, came to see me. One of the police surrounding us broke rank on the last day to shake our hands."

Unfortunately, despite activists' best efforts, repeated proposals to the IWC for South Pacific and South Atlantic whale sanctuaries have never reached the 75 percent approval needed to pass. Howie concluded, "If Japan weren't buying off smaller countries, the IWC would be more of a conservation body than a whaling one. Now it's fifty-fifty. This year, 2018, Brazil and the South American bloc is hopeful to finally achieve the South Atlantic Whale Sanctuary at the IWC in Florianópolis."

Howie would return to Japan a few years later as a result of posing a question to Australian professional free surfer Dave Rastovich, who resided in the same small community: "Why is it that the international surf media never talks about the killing of whales and dolphins? Are there any people closer to dolphins than surfers?" Dave looked at him and asked, "Dolphins are being killed?" He couldn't believe it. Howie informed him of the slaughters taking place off Japan, Peru, the Faroes Islands, Iceland, Norway, and the Antarctic, and Dave became inspired to join forces with him and do something about it. Together, they formed S4C at the next IWC, in Sorrento, Italy, in 2004, to bring awareness to the global surfing, diving, and sailing communities about dolphin slaughters, whaling, and other marine life issues.

S4C traveled to the "killing cove" in Taiji, Japan, where thousands of dolphins are slaughtered annually, and certain dolphins are selected to be sold alive into captivity. After a standoff of over a week that saw the slaughter suspended due to their presence, the group of twenty-two S4C members held a peaceful ceremony for the dolphins—fellow "surfers"—that were murdered there. Angry fishermen looked on, wanting the surfers and the publicity they might garner gone so they could continue working.

S4C members left for Osaka to catch return flights home, but on being informed that a pod of pilot whales had been corralled into the cove and was being butchered, some of the crew drove through the night to paddle back out at dawn. Even though they'd known the killing would resume at some point in time, they were close enough to the cove this time to feel they had a chance at saving some of the cetaceans' lives.

What had been a green-water bay the day before was now a blood bath. The water was colored red by the recent slaughter; some of the animals were still alive, spyhopping and crying out in distress. This time the six surfers maintaining a peaceful circle near the slaughter were aggressively confronted by the fisherman, some of whom used sharp fishing sticks to push the surfers away. The fishermen were irate about the interruption to their business and about the film crews, including ones from CNN, who were recording.

Regretfully, S4C was forced to leave for their safety, but their footage from the event made its way into international media, from surfing networks to the award-winning documentaries *The Cove* and *Minds in the Water*, both of which exposed the brutal reality of dolphin and whale slaughter to millions of people worldwide.

Although known mostly for its Taiji action, S4C doesn't seek to be constantly radical. "We simply choose our moments when we can turn up and be effective," Howie explained. "We believe education, fun, working alongside other groups, sharing story, music, and inspired art to be equally important."

As a small organization, S4C has collaborated with like-minded organizations. For example, in 2006, S4C joined forces with the International Fund for Animal Welfare (IFAW) and the Oceana Project to create the Humpback Whale Icon Project, an idea of Howie's. Coastal towns throughout Australia participated in creating awareness and empathy for the Eastern and Western Seaboard humpbacks by each "adopting" one of the whales that migrate along these shores. This acknowledgment serves to honor the distinct identity of each whale (scientists catalog them by their unique tail fluke markings). About sixty-five towns celebrate a known and named whale since the project's inception through wide-ranging activities during the annual return of the humpback whales.

Whether he's at direct action events or creating a line of banners outside IWC meetings, Howie tells the media, "We are here representing the entire international surfing community against the killing of whales and dolphins, and that community numbers into the tens of millions." He added, "I've never had a surfer come up to me and say, 'Hey, not in my name!'" Everyone seems glad to be represented in this way.

Howie's activism returned to art after he was approached by Women for Whales, a collective of ocean advocates, to make a statement on behalf of S4C against fracking proposals for the Algarve coast of Portugal. "I said I would come and make a statement if they would find me a wall." He chuckled. To Howie, a wall is one large canvas. He was offered a fifteen-meter wall in Lagos, Portugal. Adhering to his personal artist philosophy "where there's a wall, there's a whale," he painted a sperm whale ripping an oil platform out of the sea and completed the mural with the phrase "Oil and water don't mix," written in Portuguese. Passersby cheered the final result, and the mayor has asked him to return and paint the rest of the nearly two-hundred-meter wall. "And I plan to!" Howie grinned.

At this point in his life, Howie is trying to transition out of direct activism and more into his own art and music. "There are so many passionate young people with unique skills I don't have, who are forging ahead as shark defenders or game changers in regard to the plastics issue, renewable energy systems, and community sustainability. I might still have the passion, but we need to have new crew to be even more effective into the future.

"What I tell kids in schools is that it's very easy to assume that someone else is doing what's needed, someone else is taking care of something, someone else is more qualified, but in fact, if you feel strongly about some situation and you want to do something positive about it, you're the right person in the right place at the right time."

Howie pointed out that Project Jonah started in the USA in the 1970s with hundreds and then thousands of school kids writing letters against whaling, and that effort had a huge effect—it was a major impetus for countries to create Marine Mammal Protection Acts. Howie also reminds kids that such critical achievements during the 1970s and '80s were carried out without the aid of the internet. If people could do what they did without that tool, we can certainly do our part with its helpful reach.

In any talk Howie gives at schools not only does he encourage students to take pride in and ownership of their local and marine environment, he also has lateral ideas on how we use language. "For example, I might tell them they can refuse the title of 'nonsmokers,' given we are 'breathers.' I don't define myself by what I don't do; smoking is an aberration of breathing, not the other way around. I suggest to them to stay with the whale and dolphin tribe and be breathers."

He likes to play with shifts in perspectives in other ways as well. While being interviewed for *Totally Wild*, an Australian TV show for kids, he said, "A lot of people think that because this reef is in front of Sydney, a city of four million people, it's normal to be impacted by litter. But I say it should be cleaner, because we have four million people to keep it clean.

"In the end, given how we are all caught in this imperfect life together being imperfect beings together, I have a little saying that I remind myself with from time to time, which is: 'not enough time to do everything, plenty of time to do anything, just enough time to do something.'" With a wry grin, he added, "And another one I wrote brings me back to where my own journey began: 'when in life ~ breathe; when in search ~ walk; when in love ~ swim.'"

To learn more about Surfers for Cetaceans, visit www.s4cglobal.org.

ODIN LONNING AND ANN STATELER: *A Native Perspective*

Odin Lonning and Ann Stateler are like song and dance. Each offers an estimable energy of his and her own, but together their contributions are incendiary. The two met in a serendipitous fashion while on Vashon Island, Washington. "Orca Annie," as Ann became known while interning at the Whale Museum on San Juan Island, was already immersed in all things killer whale. She moved to Vashon from San Juan Island in 1994 to continue studying the remarkable cetacean. As a marine naturalist and environmental educator of Choctaw/Five Tribes descent, she saw a hole in messaging around killer whale conservation: Indigenous perspectives were not included in the narrative.

When Ann saw a postcard for an art show opening that had an image of a killer whale fin drum on it, she knew she had to meet the artist. The artist, Odin, is an award-winning Tlingit artist, heritage specialist, and traditional dancer. He was visiting Vashon Island to help carve totem poles and put on an art show. The two proved to be "immediately simpatico" and began collaborating on original educational presentations that blend Native science, culture, and art.

One of their primary goals is to bring awareness to the similarities between Native Northwest cultures and Northwest Coast orca societies and to specify ways individuals and communities can protect and honor the imperiled orcas of the Salish Sea.

Odin has his mother to thank for putting him on the path of pursuing Native culture and art. He was born into Tlingit culture in Juneau, Alaska, but it wasn't until she brought him to a performance by a traditional dance group when he was ten that the "pride hairs" on the back of his neck stood up and forced him to pay attention. Seeing elders dressed in traditional regalia—that had likely been passed on from their ancestors—struck him as extremely powerful.

On his own accord, he began studying the art and culture of the Tlingit. His family encouraged his new-found interest by giving him books on the topic for his birthday and Christmas. He trained his eyes to recognize the symbols for each animal, including the killer whale, which was represented by its dorsal fin, tail, and head and teeth.

What began as only a general interest naturally evolved into something deeper. "I had a knack for copying and learning how to do designs, but eventually I realized that doing the art makes sense only if I know the culture behind the artwork," he said. To further explore the culture, he joined a dance group in Juneau in 1992. Through traditional songs, he learned words and phrases in the native tongue of his tribe.

In discussions with elders, he came to understand that nothing is compartmentalized in Native cultures—the songs, stories, dances, and artwork are all interrelated. And the foundation for all aspects of Native cultures is respect for animals and nature and an understanding of what nature and animals have to teach us. Interestingly, some of the more impressive stories he heard were about human and killer whale interactions. Many of those stories, however, are not shared outside of Native clans.

Odin's own first experience with the species came when, as a young teenager, he was out salmon fishing with his father and his uncle northwest of Juneau. "I have a vivid memory of coming around the point of Admiralty Island, which is a very wild area with traditional Native villages, and seeing a pod of orcas. They were probably about a quarter-mile away, but close enough to see tall fins and blows."

He began to notice that the killer whale appeared in Coastal Native cultures everywhere—from petroglyphs along the outer coast of Washington State to totem poles and family crests. His own artwork incorporated the image, on drums he painted and boxes he carved, but his knowledge about the species and its complex societies wasn't much until he met Orca Annie in 1999.

Although she had been living in Arizona, Ann had an interest in the marine environment. She moved to San Juan Island in 1992 to participate in an internship at the Whale Museum. She'd expected to be exposed to Native culture and art but instead heard and saw very little—until she visited Vancouver Island, British Columbia. By the time a serious decline in the Southern Resident killer whale population began in 1997, she had realized how important it was to have Native perspective included in education surrounding conservation—Native societies historically lived in greater harmony with nature.

After meeting Odin, she came up with the idea to collaborate on a presentation called *Kéet Shuká*, which is a Tlingit phrase that roughly translates as "killer whale ancestors, descendants, and their images in crests, stories, and art." The presentation integrates Tlingit regalia, song, dance, stories, and Odin's artwork with video and photographic teaching tools. The underlying intention of *Kéet Shuká* is to illuminate the spiritual and ecological significance of the killer whale in the Pacific Northwest, to detail the threats facing the whales, and to suggest ways to protect them.

"When we do *Kéet Shuká*, I try to get people to imagine what it was like pre-contact for people who traveled primarily by water for trading, hunting, or potlatching in other villages," Odin shared. "The water was our highway, so if you're on the water that much, you're likely to have a very close relationship with the killer whale."

He went on to share his philosophy on just how close of a relationship he feels the two species must have had—one where communication was possible. "There are many stories going way back in time of First Nations people learning from killer whales by watching them and through their interactions with them. I personally have a theory that if you go back in time far enough, all humans had some basic ability to telepathically communicate with animals—not with words, but with images and emotion."

He continued, "If you talk to Indigenous people, regardless of what tribe, you'll hear stories about a medicine person or a shaman who had certain abilities other people did not, one of which was to communicate directly with animals—which is where the stories come from." Such stories are accepted among Native peoples as "the way things were." It is clear when listening to them being related by elders that they're not "exaggerating or lying."

In contemporary non-Native society, people like to write off stories of, for example, "a shaman visiting a killer whale's undersea village" as fanciful or cute and unrealistic. Odin believes that although such a visit may not have happened physically, the shaman may have been able to spiritually go undersea through bilocation—a psychic or miraculous ability for an individual to be located in two places at the same time. It is a possibility Western science is starting to open up to, but Odin is skeptical that the ancient ability still exists.

"I think that ability is gone now. There might be rare instances where [bilocation] is still alive, and if so, I think it would be with Indigenous people. With the so-called progression of the human race, people are increasingly disconnected from nature. Everybody is so attached to their devices that knowing how to watch and listen to nature doesn't exist anymore. But that's what I'm excited to impart through teaching—how to go back to that language of gratitude and respect for animals and nature."

Odin and Ann have staged *Kéet Shuká* for diverse audiences along the West Coast, from Glacier Bay, Alaska, to San Diego, California. Venues have included classrooms, conferences, museums, Northwest Folklife and other festivals, senior centers, culture camps for Native students, and Native art events. The presentation evolves with each new audience and adapts accordingly when performed for nonprofit groups such as the American Cetacean Society, People for Puget Sound, Project Seawolf, and the Whale Museum.

Odin's artwork is another way to educate the public about issues that concern him. He has carved visual messages into totem poles, boxes, wall panels, masks, paddles, and bowls. He paints original designs on drums, canvas, paper, wood, and leather. He has even etched glass and copper and designed Native regalia with appliqué and leather.

Although he began creating art as a teenager, he received his first major art commission at the age of twenty from Sealaska Native Corporation in Juneau. After Odin relocated to Washington, he received a grant to carve a seven-foot-wide cutout red cedar panel for the Seattle Aquarium. The piece depicts five different killer whale designs; each design is done in a distinct tribal style, calling attention to how many tribes honor and revere the killer whale. "I started with Alaska and came all the way down here to the Salish people. The piece makes a positive statement about the Native connection," he said. The panel is part of a permanent Puget Sound orcas exhibit and was envisioned to incorporate Native perspective into the bigger picture.

Odin's largest killer-whale-specific commission is the carving of a twenty-foot-long, nine-foot-high killer whale sculpture he completed for Everett Community College. Mounted on two metal posts, the whale sits horizontally and has a thunderbird sitting on its back. The totem was derived from a concept by a former faculty member who was also Tlingit.

Throughout his artistic career, Odin has learned the role that metaphor plays in traditional oratory, known as "potlatch oratory." The term relates to the ceremonial gathering of Northwest Coast Native peoples where possessions are given to display wealth or enhance prestige. Potlatches still happen today, and storytelling is a key component of the ceremonies. Odin explained, "One of the valued skills of a speaker for a chief at a potlatch is the ability to address and entertain an audience, which is done by inserting little jokes and metaphors and often saying three different things within one sentence."

Metaphor isn't only expressed through spoken word, however. Visual art can incorporate the figure of speech as well. Totem poles, for example, are known for storytelling. There's a Coastal Native tradition that existed in British Columbia and Alaska when it comes to styles of poles. "Ridicule poles" were erected for the purpose of scorning somebody who deserved to be publicly shamed. An early example was carved to shame a chief who did not pay back a debt. The person being ridiculed was indicated on the pole by being held upside-down by the feet by an animal that was related to the clan ridiculing that person.

The tradition has largely died out, but it resurrects every now and then. In 2007, on the eighteenth anniversary of the Exxon Valdez oil spill in Prince William Sound, Alaska, a ridicule pole was unveiled that mocked Exxon Mobil Corporation for breaking its promise to pay affected Alaskans billions of dollars in punitive damages. Designed by Alutiiq and Tlingit carver Mike Webber, the seven-foot-tall totem bears the upside-down face of the former Exxon Mobil CEO sporting a Pinocchio-like nose. Other images painted on the pole include a killer whale spouting oil from his blowhole, as well as a sea duck, a sea otter, and an eagle floating dead in oil.

"I've been tempted to make little political statements with my art as well," Odin shared. At the top of his agenda is to insert images that reflect his personal view of how people treat killer whales. He stated his recent desire to incorporate more activism into his artwork, whether to symbolize his respect for nature and animals, to emphasize the need for conservation, or to protest a political decision.

There are a couple of topics that get Odin and Ann equally riled up. One is the issue of captivity. They compare capturing orcas— stealing young family members—for the purpose of placing them in a pool for human entertainment to the historical practice of taking First Nations children and placing them in residential schools. They view their relationship to orcas as protectors.

The duo was instrumental in the rehabilitation of the orphaned and emaciated Northern Resident orca known as Springer, who spent six months hanging out at the north end ferry dock of Vashon Island in 2002. Ann lovingly refers to Springer as their "foster child." She shared, "Historically, it's a really big deal if a killer whale appears near your village. The orca would be considered a messenger. There are many places Springer could have camped out instead, but she picked a good place because she had us here watching out for her every day, along with our friend Mark Sears, a

West Seattle–based whale researcher, and other people deeply interested in her welfare."

Among those watching out for her were biologists who identified her family pod by listening to her vocalizations on a hydrophone. They determined her mother had recently died, which directly contributed to her separation from her pod. However, "not everybody was respecting her wildness," Ann explained. She said some people would intentionally try to interact with her and even feed her human food.

Finally, the United States National Marine Fisheries Service (NMFS) made a decision to capture her and try to reintegrate her into her pod. She would be moved to a sea pen off Manchester, Washington, first, where she would receive medical treatment before being transported to a sea pen near Johnstone Strait, British Columbia, where her family frequently visited at that time of year.

A ceremonial sendoff was organized the day before she was moved from Vashon waters, which was attended by Odin and Ann and members of a Tlingit dance group. After arriving at Dong Chong Bay in Canadian waters, she was greeted by the Namgis First Nation band, who arrived in canoes with their chief, who was dressed in traditional regalia. "They came out to greet her as a returning relative, welcoming her back to her ancestral waters." Ann smiled. Odin and Ann hope Springer's situation brings to light that the sacred relationship between Native cultures and killer whales is not merely an ancient one.

Springer wouldn't stay in her new sea pen for long. Her first night there, she heard her family's calls on the hydrophone. She started vocalizing excitedly, and the following day, when her pod showed up near her pen, the decision was made to release her. Springer has been observed in Johnstone Strait several times in subsequent years, traveling with her pod. She thus became the only orca in history to be successfully reintegrated into a wild population after human intervention. Not only did she reintegrate, she's helping her pod repopulate. She was seen with a new calf in 2013 and another in 2017, who was confirmed by a research survey to be her second offspring.

In addition to using killer whales for entertainment in captivity, another human behavior that concerns Odin and Ann is excessive boat-based whale watching. "When do the orcas get a break?" Odin asked. "There never used to be winter whale watching down here. Now there is. How is it acceptable to hound killer whales all day long regardless of where they go?" He shared his philosophy that real-time sighting networks can be responsible for applying more pressure on an already-endangered population. "We have witnessed bad boating behavior so many times by people who were following online as to where the whales were headed."

Odin added that it has been scientifically proven that vessel noise can be detrimental to orcas, causing stress and interfering with hunting techniques needed for survival. There are also numerous incidents of ship strikes, with Resident killer whales sustaining gashes from contact with boat propellers. "Does there have to be blood in the water before any changes are made?" he asked.

He shared that the worst behavior he's seen by boaters "wanting a Kodak moment" was the harassment of a mother and frail baby calf. Ann added that mainstream society has become so attached to technology that people ignore the significance of the present moment—missing the opportunity to connect on a more visceral level with an ancient and fascinating species in exchange for snapping a photo. Furthermore, knowing where the whales are in advance detracts from the wonder of encountering them fortuitously. "There's nothing like a surprise visit," she added. "It's a peak experience when they show up unexpected."

That experience is heightened when one considers the ephemeral aspect of the population of Resident orcas that call the Salish Sea home. "I came [to the Pacific Northwest] full of wonder and hope in 1992 to study a flourishing population. It is heartbreaking to me that this many years on, I might be witnessing an extinction," Ann considered.

The passing of Granny, a Southern Resident killer whale matriarch who died in late 2016 at the approximate age of ninety years, was already a difficult loss for Ann. "She was so significant to the Southern Resident community, and to me. I knew her for twenty-five years, and it truly felt like losing a granny or auntie when she died."

To Ann—and to a lot of whale lovers and researchers—Granny's passing represented the end of an era. "Every orca is special and valuable, but especially the elders. When they die, they leave a big hole in the community. There's a parallel in Native communities where when you lose an elder, you lose encyclopedic knowledge—not to mention all the other important social functions they perform."

Granny's time may simply have come, but for the remaining members of her pod and those of the other Resident killer whale populations, time is running out for humans to make choices that prevent them from dying out prematurely. "People need to step up and do what needs to be done," Ann said passionately. "And much of what needs to be done is difficult and is going to demand some sacrifice from all of us. To me, there's been a total imbalance of sacrifice; the Southern Residents have been making all of the sacrifices in the worst ways: the loss of their family members, their territory, the quality of their habitat, and the food they eat. What sacrifices are humans going to make?"

Ann went on to list a variety of threats facing the Southern Residents today: depleted Chinook salmon stocks in the North Pacific; deadly toxins in their blubber; stress from ever-increasing underwater noise and crowding by boats; disease; oil spills; wholesale effects of climate change.

She further noted problems affecting endangered Chinook salmon, a favorite food of the Southern Residents, which include outmoded dams that impede fish passage (and not just the more notorious Lower Snake River dams but damaged floodgates on the Fraser River and Klamath River dams). Excessive logging and global warming cause the temperatures of streams to rise and imperil the survivability of juvenile salmon.

Sacrifices Ann recommends include eating less meat—or no meat—and not eating farmed salmon. "Also, don't waste food, because there are so many resources involved in making food," she suggested. "No one wants to ask anyone to make a sacrifice, but sacrifice is required if we really care about these orcas not going extinct. And don't just do one thing; do *more* than one thing."

In their educational presentations, Odin and Ann emphasize that Western scientific strategies are not enough to truly appreciate and advocate for these animals. "Science is important, but more attention needs to be placed on understanding killer whales behaviorally. They're very psychologically sophisticated, and our knowledge deficit is in understanding their culture and social dynamics. How do they function as a First Nation in the water, as a community unto themselves? They have their own ceremonies and rituals that are obviously very important to them and about which we know very little."

A population of killer whales going extinct is like having a human First Nation or tribe going extinct, they believe. "As a cultural educator and a teaching artist, what I hope to pass on to my students is to have the same attitude as we do—that the whales going extinct is unacceptable," Odin shared.

Ann concluded, "Killer whales are smart enough to know they have to deal with our species somehow. Their fate is in our hands to some degree because humans have been so destructive to their habitat, so they understand that there needs to be some form of coexistence."

In Tlingit tradition, the killer whale is viewed as a special protector of humankind and has never been hunted. Perhaps it's time we become special protectors of killer whales. If we take note of their role as guides, we too will understand the need for coexistence.

For more information on Odin's artwork and on Odin and Orca Annie's cultural presentations, visit www.odinlonning.com. Photo by Erin Corra.

V
NOISE AND CHEMICAL POLLUTION

Noise and chemical pollution threaten every species that calls the ocean home—as well as land-dwelling humans too. To understand the impact boat noise can have on marine mammals, consider a statistic revealed in the documentary *Sonic Sea*: A long-term study of East Coast Right whales revealed a significant reduction in stress hormones at a particular time in history—the days following the 9/11 attacks when security measures halted nonessential marine traffic. Stress levels returned to "normal" after the travel ban was lifted.

Just because we can't hear underwater boat noise doesn't mean it's quiet. Cars or trucks that produced so much sound would be banned. Propellers produce some of the loudest continuous sounds in the ocean: over 170 decibels from large ships and even 145 to 160 decibels from small, fast-traveling pleasure boats. These sounds can significantly impair the ability for both toothed and baleen whales to communicate and hunt prey.

And that's just noise from propellers and engines. Navy sonar takes noise pollution to a whole new level. Military boats conduct training exercises using low-frequency sonar in inland waters and off coasts—within the same vocal range that orcas use to communicate. Shock waves from this level of noise can deafen or even kill a nearby whale. It can also confuse any number of cetaceans near the blasts; mass strandings (when cetaceans strand themselves on land) of many different species of whales have been proven to be the result of navy sonar testing. (The US Navy has only admitted responsibility for one—a mass beaked whale stranding in The Bahamas in 2000.)

Seismic testing used in oil exploration is another major threat; the air guns used to search for offshore oil and gas are loud enough to kill marine life—and they are used as often as every ten seconds, twenty-four hours a day, for days and weeks at a time. Seismic air guns are also the first step toward habitat destruction, oil spills, and ocean acidification and are considered a contribution to climate change—if underwater oil is found, offshore drilling and oil transport and its risks begin.

Noise pollution also occurs as a result of the near constant whale watching industry. NOAA (National Oceanic and Atmospheric Administration) reports that the number of registered whale watching boats between the United States and Canada has increased from seventy-six in 2010 to ninety-six in 2018. Plus, there are countless recreational boaters who contribute to underwater noise and the creation of underwater obstacle courses. Kayaks are the least obtrusive watercraft, but even these can be startling for whales and difficult to maneuver around.

Finally, for those cetaceans who frequent the Salish Sea, not only do they have to contend with the eleven thousand large vessels (oil tankers, container ships, and bulk cargo carriers) that transit through these waters each year but they are facing an expansion of the Kinder Morgan Trans Mountain Pipeline System, which will increase oil tanker traffic out of Vancouver, British Columbia, from seventy-one ships in 2010 to over four hundred ships per year. Such an increase in traffic makes two dangers inevitable: ship strikes and oil spills.

The pipelines claim that precautions are taken to avoid oil spills and damage to the ecosystem, but their track record isn't very convincing. Fourteen oil spills occurred between 1995 and 2008 from tankers in Washington State, releasing nearly fourteen thousand gallons of oil in and around the Salish Sea. Within that same period, 132 near-miss incidents also occurred, which combined, would have released nearly 3 billion gallons of oil. In other words, it's not a matter of *if* a potentially catastrophic spill will occur but *when*.

Nearly one-third of the Resident orcas who were exposed to the 1989 Exxon Valdez oil spill in Prince William Sound, Alaska, died within a year. That statistic offers little hope for the Resident orcas and other marine life that call the Salish Sea home. And of course, those aren't the only populations subject to contamination in our waters.

There is a "dead zone" in the Gulf of Mexico—an area of low oxygen that can kill fish and marine life—that is about the size of New Jersey. This dead zone was caused mostly by Midwestern farms whose fertilizer was carried downstream by the Mississippi River. Then there is the Great Pacific Garbage Patch, about a thousand miles off the coast of California. It is a floating dump of an estimated 3.5 million tons of garbage—at least 80 percent of which is plastic.

It is no wonder that, as apex predators at the top of the food chain, killer whales rank among the world's most contaminated marine mammals. They consume the toxins that animals all down the food chain consumed. Sadly, these ingested toxins are passed directly to calves through their mother's milk and fat stores— making the mother less toxic due to offloading, and the calf more likely to die.

There are many additional ocean pollutants besides oil, plastics, and fertilizer runoff; industrial waste, dioxins from the pulp and paper bleaching process, polychlorinated biphenyls (PCBs) (which usually come from older electrical equipment), and waste from cruise ships all contribute to the degradation of marine habitat and marine mammal health. All of these pollutants have the potential to enter into the food chain, affecting not only marine mammals but all beings on the planet.

MEEGAN CORCORAN: *A Sea of Sound*

When considering all that she's accomplished in her career, it would be natural to assume Meegan Corcoran is far beyond her thirties. Her eclectic background spans from serving eight years in the US Navy to earning an undergraduate degree in aquatic and fisheries sciences and a master's in marine and environmental affairs. She has worked as a naturalist on whale watching boats, worked on Discovery's *Shark Week*, and currently serves as marine operations manager for the University of Washington.

Amid all her studies and careers, she has remained an outspoken advocate for developing protocols that minimize the harmful effects of navy sonar training and testing on marine mammals. She loved her time in the navy—she is by no means a critic of the institution itself—but she believes it's necessary to find a balance between national security and environmental health. Her master's thesis was written on multiple ways the latter could be achieved.

Her youthful enthusiasm is preeminent, but she has lived long enough to sometimes sound like a cynic. Having just read Alan Weisman's book *The World without Us*, she is beginning to believe the planet would be much better off if humans simply ceased to exist. That consideration, however, doesn't keep her from striving to educate others on how our species can—and must—find a middle ground.

Meegan has never shied away from challenging authority. As a young adult, she told her mother she wanted to be a marine biologist. Her mother told her she would never make any money in the field, but Meegan retaliated by pointing to the National Geographic show on TV and saying, "Those people are doing it, so why can't I?"

She had done the same as a five-year-old. While watching *Shark Week* on the Discovery Channel, she pointed to the screen and said, "That's what I want to do!" Her mother replied, "You want to be a shark researcher?" Young Meegan replied, "Yes!" Perhaps her mother had found the claim easy to dismiss at the time. But her daughter's desire proved to not simply be a phase. It was an obsession.

Not that it wasn't encouraged in some ways. Meegan grew up in Southern California, only fourteen miles from the beach. Her interest in the ocean developed naturally due to early and regular exposure but also because of several family trips to SeaWorld and Hawaii. She regularly saw dolphins in the wild and swam with them at the Hilton in Honolulu. She didn't know enough to challenge those institutions at the time, or no doubt she would have. Though she stated she was always an environmentalist, she didn't become an activist until after she joined the US Navy.

Meegan graduated high school just before the 9/11 terrorist attacks. Until then, she had never even entertained the idea of joining the military; she was on track to study marine biology.

"I felt compelled to do something [for the country], like a lot of other people," she explained. "I was nineteen, and I was like, 'Let's go!'" From the start, she didn't really understand what she had signed up for. She was surprised to discover she could pick her own job. "I thought you just joined the navy and were a sailor." She laughed. There were over sixty job descriptions for Meegan to read through. She was helped with her decision when she shared that she was into whales and dolphins. Navy representatives replied, "Perfect! You should be a sonar technician because you can train dolphins!"

She couldn't believe her great fortune. At first. "That was only 99 percent of a lie," she went on to clarify, "because there *are* four sonar technicians who train dolphins in the navy." Unfortunately, she would not be one of them. Instead, she was commissioned to deploy low-frequency active sonar (LFA) into the water—which had the potential to kill whales and dolphins.

When she learned of that danger, she was horrified. She started extensively researching the topic and discovered that the navy had recently admitted responsibility for what marine mammal scientists had suspected for decades. There was too much evidence to deny that the mass stranding of seventeen marine mammals in The Bahamas (one of which washed ashore outside the island home of Center for Whale Research founder Ken Balcomb) in March 2000 was a result of the coinciding use of active midrange sonar by navy ships.

Before and since that conclusion, several other mass strandings have occurred in correlation with navy sonar tests. Beaked whales are the most affected, as they are deeper and longer divers. Some of the more famous incidents include: fifteen Cuvier's beaked whales stranding in northern Italy (1963); twenty beaked whales of multiple species stranding in the Canary Islands (1989); and fourteen Cuvier's beaked whales stranding in Greece (1996).

Tissue samples were collected from four dead whales in The Bahamas that revealed signs of massive hemorrhaging, bleeding in the inner ears as well as bleeding around the brain, both of which can be caused by exceptionally loud noises. The adage "a deaf whale is a dead whale" applied in this case. Meegan wasn't involved in that training exercise from two years earlier, but nonetheless she felt incredibly guilty. "I wasn't quiet about the conflict, that's for sure. I was the resident environmentalist on board the navy ship."

In a 2016 talk at San Juan Island's Superpod gathering of orca enthusiasts, she shared a picture of herself wearing a helmet with a sticker reading, *Save the Whales, Stop LFA NOW!*, while deploying active sonar. Her colleagues would make "jokes" about the situation, such as suggesting eating whale burgers for dinner. They were trying to make light of something they reluctantly felt they had no control over. "It was heartbreaking," Meegan recalled.

She kept asking herself, "How can we do this?" She became really interested in policy—one, how it's legal to deploy sonar that can kill even endangered species, and two, what regulations existed to monitor that danger. She found out that the National

Oceanic and Atmospheric Association (NOAA) did have a lot of limitations on where sonar could be used and how many times per year, all of which were based on the migratory paths of whales. "But those regulations don't negate the fact that it still harms marine mammals, because the whales can be absolutely anywhere at any time," she said.

Unfortunately, they weren't ever anywhere Meegan could see them until, while she was stationed on Whidbey Island, Washington, her sister came for a visit and the two decided to go whale watching. At the time, boats only had to stay at a distance of one hundred yards from whales (now it is two hundred yards). Meegan therefore had an up-close and personal encounter with the Southern Resident killer whales. Although, for Meegan, it wasn't close enough.

"My sister was literally holding my belt loop, so I wouldn't fall off the boat. I was in awe; it was unbelievable. They are such majestic creatures and they have such amazing energy. I was a little bit in disbelief when I saw them; I couldn't believe that moment was happening. All I wanted to do was get closer. I wanted to connect. I always knew I was into whales but didn't know how much until I saw them."

Although Meegan never personally saw a whale or dolphin injured as a result of sonar, she is quick to clarify that most of the time, you don't. "When you find beached whales of multiple species, as was the case in The Bahamas, you can assume that's just the tip of the iceberg as far as animals who were harmed."

Despite the internal conflict, Meegan completed her four-year commitment to the navy. She knew she wanted to use what she had learned during her service to become an advocate for the whales, but she soon discovered she needed to gather more information. The navy was just about to switch to a new sonar system, and she realized she would need to understand it to determine what advocacy work could be done. Six months later, she rejoined the navy for nearly another four years.

The choice wasn't a hardship for her. "I loved the navy; I really did." Her face lit up. "I had so much fun traveling the world and making dear friends. It was just that one thing that bothered me—the fact that, environmentally, it was horrible." After completing her second period of service in the navy, she felt equipped to tackle some of those practices she knew were detrimental to marine life.

By this time, she had completed an undergraduate degree through the University of Washington in aquatic and fisheries sciences. Now, she would return to the school to study marine law and policy and obtain a master's degree in the field. Her thesis was on five ways to use sonar without hurting marine mammals. Her goal was to demonstrate to the US Navy that it could maintain national security while lowering environmental harm.

Outlined in her proposal were strategies such as: designating a marine mammal identifier who is trained to listen for (acoustically detect) marine mammals; lowering sonar volume (decibel level), especially since it's not necessary to fully deploy sonar when only training; increasing simulated training while decreasing training that uses sonar pings, thus greatly limiting the sound projected into the water; conducting sonar tests further offshore and holding one longer training session instead of several shorter ones; and raising volume slowly (ramp-up period) so that anything in range has time to move away.

After she wrote her thesis, she started consulting with the National Resources Defense Council. She explained how there are several environmental attorneys that take the navy to court all the time. Many of the cases she consulted on the council ended up winning; the navy has since then been changing the ways sonar is used.

She humbly explained, "There are a lot of people fighting the navy's use of sonar, but where I came in is I had personal knowledge of how their systems work. Plus, I had a master's degree in marine law, so that gave me a little bit of clout in the conversation." There is still a lot of work to be done, she knows. Having been out of the navy for nearly as long as she had been in, she knew from friends still serving that the systems had changed yet again.

"Some of my navy friends have come to my environmental talks. They feel the same way as me. We're all of a similar mindset, the same generation that asks, 'Wait, we're killing all of these things for what?'" Meegan has since decreased the number of sonar talks she gives, since there is so much she no longer knows about the navy's system. "I still know the basics, but I don't want to be naïve and give out false information."

She feels, however, that she did everything she could with what she did know to make a difference. Of course, her knowledge about sonar still extends far beyond the average person's. "Most people have no idea about sonar." She shook her head. Even though the waters off the Washington coast host a sonar testing and training range that is the size of the state of California and directly in the zone of impact for the endangered Southern Resident killer whales, "the information is just not even out there."

Meegan is still passionate about the topic, but her priorities have shifted. She knows that the navy invests millions of dollars every year to figure out the active sonar/marine mammal problem. "They're listening; things are changing. Of course, it is in their best interest to discover newer technologies." She has therefore decided to use her education and experience in a variety of other ways; one of her career highlights was working as a fisheries biologist for the University of Washington. She studied Chinook salmon in the Columbia River to determine if the wild Chinook were breeding with hatchery Chinook. They were.

"That realization was really big because it was affecting policy," she shared. "People say we need more hatcheries in order to have more fish, but what we really need is to take down dams and give the fish back their spawning grounds." It's another topic she is passionate about. "We don't want to have hatchery fish make wild fish more unfit. If we have any chance at all at preventing wild fish from going extinct, we can't keep putting in hatcheries."

Later, she moved to San Juan Island and began working as a naturalist on whale watching boats. That's when she really started to learn about the species of whales in the area: the humpback, minke, gray whales, and orca. "Now I see whales all the time, but

I've never, ever taken it for granted. The whales almost feel like family in a way, because there's specific individuals that I see a lot. I know their life history, who's related to who, and so forth."

She's also been witness to some pretty remarkable interactions between whales and humans. "There's a gal who is a repeat customer with a whale watching company here who is part Native American. Every time she's on the boat, the whales swim right up to her. It's amazing. One time, she was sitting on the bow when a whale came up and lifted its head up out of the water, vocalizing right at her."

She shared that the Southern Resident orcas also respond uniquely to whale researcher Ken Balcomb. "I don't know if they recognize him or the boat, but whichever it is, they know he is someone that cares deeply about them. They greet him every time—especially if they haven't seen him for a while—by swimming right up to the boat or going under his boat and breaching. We don't see that really with anyone else."

As an occasional captain for whale watching boats, Meegan adheres to the policy of offering the whales considerable distance from the boat. "People would harass these animals if there weren't regulations. I don't know of a single case of a wild animal being habituated to humans that has survived. There are those that love the animal, but then there are those who are scared. And if they're scared, they kill it." The latter is a sad reality of the nature of our species.

After working as a naturalist for two years, Meegan was hired on at the University of Washington's marine lab in Friday Harbor as the manager of marine operations. She facilitates the research vessel program: "I help scientists and student researchers come up with ways to get the data they need, whether that's biological data of critters or oceanographic data."

She continues to promote education in additional ways—sometimes still on the topic of sonar. She manages a Facebook page (Sonar and Cetacean Mitigation Effort) to notify followers of when it's time to voice opinions to NOAA. Every five years, the US Navy must renew its permits. NOAA is the permitting agency, and a public comment period is required. She also gives occasional talks at schools on sonar and whales and on great white sharks.

Another notable characteristic of Meegan's resume is she studied great white sharks in South Africa alongside two of her heroes: shark biologists Ryan Johnson and Chris Follows. The opportunity led to her being invited to help with an episode of *Shark Week* (called "Ultimate Air Jaws"). It was Meegan's job to lure the sharks close to the boat for filming by throwing chum into the water.

There may not be space for these types of distinguishing experiences on her resume, but she has also swum with humpback whales and looked into the eye of a whale. "In *Moby Dick*, they say that once you look into the eye of a whale, you're never the same. It's kind of true; it's a phenomenal experience." When asked to further describe what she felt, she added, "The real feeling is one of honor—that they looked at *you*. It's like having a superstar take a moment to connect with you. You can really see how intelligent they are. They're rock stars."

That experience only increased the level of amazement she feels for marine mammals and her commitment to caring for them. Many concerns plague her: "Shipping noise is increasing; it's only getting louder and louder underwater. These animals use sound like we use our eyes to navigate their environment. Shipping noise can be likened to us having a bright light shined into our eyes twenty-four hours a day, seven days per week."

It's not just shipping noise and navy sonar that contribute to noise in the ocean; oil exploration is even louder than navy sonar. "They use air guns to penetrate the bottom of the ocean floor. It is incredibly loud," Meegan said. "In 2008, there were over one hundred melon-headed dolphins killed in Madagascar due to Exxon Mobil oil exploration."

Climate change is another critical concern of Meegan's. "If you look at how ocean circulation happens, it's a very finite process. Ice starts to melt at the poles; then that cold water sinks and moves along to the equator before upwelling back up and creating a huge belt of nutrients that is the basis of the food chain." She continued,

"If there's no more ice to keep this nutrient belt going, then everything is going to collapse. We're already seeing it now on the coast of California. We have sea lions starving because things are shifting; they don't have the fish they've always had in that area because the water is too warm there now for them to survive.

"We're seeing Humboldt squid in Alaska, when they're usually in Southern California and Baja, Mexico. There are bottlenose dolphins—a warm-water mammal—in Puget Sound. Everything is getting displaced. The ecosystem is so delicate in the way that it's balanced that even if an algae bloom occurs one week later than usual, everything is off. That really concerns me; we're going to see more of these disruptions that are detrimental and possibly fatal to animals—land and marine."

This is where Meegan has to self-check her state of mind. It can be easy to feel hopeless amid such environmental turmoil. At such times, she reminds herself of all the good work people are doing. "I do feel like there's an awakening happening right now, even in the depths of the craziness we're in. There's been a huge paradigm shift within the whole world. We live in a country that is so far away from enlightenment, but there are many other countries rising up and getting on the forefront of alternative energy and environmental health. I think everyone's catching on to the understanding that we only have one earth to live on."

She understands that at the helm of enlightenment is education. She is aware of how many people love whales—she saw it while working on whale watching boats. But education extends well beyond fascination. Meegan believes people need to understand how intelligent whales and dolphins are. Once that realization has been made, "it really starts the whole process of really caring about these animals. And once you start caring about this one animal, you start to wonder what makes it different from this other animal. That leads you through the process of understanding how the ecosystem works."

That's when it becomes clear how even our small behaviors impact the whole ecosystem: using pesticides on our lawns, bathing with soaps that contain chemicals, and—two more significant practices Meegan deeply wishes people would limit—eating meat and having multiple children.

She may not get very far single-handedly, but she's determined to leave an army of young activists in her wake. When asked what advice she would offer to young people interested in pursuing careers working with cetaceans, her enthusiasm becomes unbridled. "Learn as much as you possibly can and take every opportunity that comes your way. Don't be afraid to say yes to what scares you; the more you say yes, the less scared you'll become. And don't worry about the money—money will come! Take the path that is most exciting to you and trust that things will fall into place."

Also, like Meegan, don't be afraid to question authority—even if it's as powerful as the US Navy.

Follow www.facebook.com/sonarmitigation *to stay updated on NOAA public comment periods.*

CRAIG MATKIN: *A Sense of What Is*

It is sometimes assumed that science and spirituality don't mix, but Craig Matkin is a compelling example of a man who has spent over forty years in the field conducting scientific research and yet maintains an active spiritual practice and perspective. It is perhaps the latter that has aided his ability to take a step back from discouraging data and great personal loss, in order to see the openings that even the most tragic situations provide.

Having been witness to the effects of the 1989 Exxon Valdez oil spill in his beloved Prince William Sound, Alaska—and later losing his wife and research partner, Eva Saulitis, to cancer—Craig has had every reason to feel dispirited. But instead, he forges ahead with focus on what he can control: his mindset. That habit has served him well. He is quick to laugh, eager to educate, and ready for a relaxing retirement.

Craig is in the process of reducing his involvement in the nonprofit organization he founded in 1981, North Gulf Oceanic Society (NGOS), although the long-term research studies he began will remain in full swing—such as on the effects of the oil spill on a population of orcas known as the AT1, or the Chugach Transients, of which only seven individuals remain. He still loves being out on the water with the whales—he rotates between homes in Alaska and Hawaii—but his passion now is to impart his experience and wisdom to the next generation (and to bask in a bit of sunshine).

The forty years Craig has spent studying whales off the coast of Alaska coincides with the forty years he's been visiting Hawaii. He wasn't just chasing whales—he was chasing the sun. "I don't do dark." He laughed. That's no surprise, considering he grew up on the California coast. He's been in and around the water since he was a child, aside from a two-year stint attending college in

Colorado, where he learned that he couldn't live in a landlocked state.

Craig would watch gray whales off the coast of California and Baja California, Mexico, as a teenager in the 1960s—before there was much interest in the "friendlies"—but his experience with whales primarily was shore-based and intermittent until he made the move to Alaska. By participating in the Alaska studies program at the University of California, Santa Cruz, while earning an undergraduate degree in biology, he made connections in Alaska that led him to working with the Alaska Department of Fish and Game.

Even though Craig studied under Ken Norris—one of the premier marine mammal researchers at the time—he never intended to work with whales. He was on track to become a fisheries research biologist. Before he could conduct research on any species, however, he needed to gain small-boat skills and become more adept at working in Alaska's rugged environment. As it turned out, his path led to working as a commercial fisherman, which presented the perfect opportunity to expand his experience on the water and unexpectedly change the path of his career.

"When I was doing fisheries research work, I had some experiences with killer whales and humpback whales that sidetracked me," he explained. His first close encounter was at the age of around twenty-one, when he was out on a kayak, "sixty miles from nowhere," working at a remote research camp. A pod of about eight killer whales came by, joined by a false killer whale (an all-black species similar in size to a killer whale but unrelated, and very rare in Alaska), which he assumed the killer whales were going to attack. Instead, they ignored the false killer whale and charged right at him.

"I'm pretty good about animals and energy, and I didn't feel any great fear, but I couldn't figure out what was going on," he related. "So, I just sat out there, and they all swam around me, in what I know now to be group resting behavior." Craig stayed with the whales for ninety minutes or so, even paddling along with them. "After that, I said, OK, I'm going to study these guys."

He earned his master's degree in zoology in 1980 at the University of Alaska, Fairbanks, with a few bumps and bruises along the way, including losing his cabin and all his possessions (including his cameras) to fire and losing what he thought would be funding for killer whale research. He studied seals and sea lions, all the while learning the fishing grounds of the Copper River. Salmon fishing on the river was just taking off, and he could see how much money was to be made. "I thought, I know how I'm going to fund my killer whale work." Commercial fishing supported his work to a degree, but not entirely—so he started the nonprofit organization NGOS and applied for grant funding.

Since the inception of NGOS, nearly all Craig's research initiatives have gone under that entity's umbrella. The organization focuses on long-term studies because marine mammals are long-lived and difficult to study, which means some of the team's earliest studies continue to this day. The group's primary research subjects include the killer whale and humpback whale populations off the coast of Alaska, both of which Craig began researching in 1977.

Due to the unique position of having had baseline data of those populations prior to the 1989 Exxon Valdez oil spill—which dumped a catastrophic 11 million gallons of oil into Prince William Sound after striking a reef—his team of researchers has been able to assess the damages wrought by the disaster. He did clarify that with so much change going on in the environment all the time—and particularly lately with climate change—part of their job is to tease out which changes are oil related and which are not.

However, here is a sample of what they have observed since the spill: The AB-pod of Resident killer whales was seen swimming in the oil and experienced a loss of thirteen of its then thirty-five members immediately or shortly after the spill. The AT1-pod of Transient killer whales had nine members disappear in the year after the spill and additional members die shortly thereafter. Today, seven individuals remain of the original twenty-two. Not a single calf has been born to the group since the spill.

Most humpback whales had not yet returned to their feeding grounds at the time of the spill, and therefore no immediate deaths of the species were recorded. Although harbor seal numbers were already in decline before the spill, they declined even further afterward. Craig shared that their numbers seem to be coming back, although not to the degree they were at before the disaster. There was no baseline data for sea lions, but they did notice a decrease in numbers after the spill. Similarly, Dall's porpoises had not been studied previously, but after the spill, they could be seen "sporting" brown chevrons on the backs of their heads from having swum through oil, and a subjective decrease was noticed for the next dozen years.

Furthermore, complications arose with herring—a popular food source for marine birds and mammals. "We saw huge mortality in the larva, egg mutations and then an outbreak of disease. Herring is in the pits, but it's still hard to tell if it's due to other factors as well." Craig added that the herring decline was further exacerbated when the Department of Fish and Game allowed a fishery to be put in place a couple years after the oil spill.

As with all oil spills, attempts were made to clean up the area after the spill—or at least make it look like a cleanup was undertaken. "The hot-water beach cleaning does more damage than it does good," Craig shared. "We all knew it, but we couldn't stop it." Only an estimated 14 percent of the oil from the spill was actually recovered. Although having been touted as world-class, the technology available to clean up an oil spill of such proportions has changed little since the 1960s, costs billions of dollars, and still fails to get the job done.

The oil and gas industry claims that chemical dispersants, such as Corexit, can be used to break the oil into smaller pieces. It should be noted that the product was developed by an oil company. Its ingredient list is a trade secret, the product has been banned by Sweden and the United Kingdom due to the potential danger it poses to workers, and it is known to kill oil-eating bacteria. Nevertheless, the Gulf of Mexico was aerial-bombed with the product after the 2010 Deepwater Horizon oil spill, which dumped

650 million liters of crude oil into its waters. After all, they had to make it look to consumers and the media like they were doing something.

That point was explored in a July 2016 *Smithsonian Magazine* article, "Why We Pretend to Clean Up Oil Spills." The article brought up that in Canada, for example, multinational oil companies also own the corporations licensed to respond to catastrophic spills. Allowing these companies to determine marine spill preparedness and response represents an obvious conflict of interest.

Responders themselves are therefore not likely to be trained scientists. After the Deepwater Horizon spill, "animal rescuers" treated oil-soaked birds with charcoal solutions, antibiotics, and dish soap before forcing them to swallow Pepto-Bismol (which helps absorb hydrocarbons). Scientists know that this type of cleaning can be as harmful to birds' immune systems as the oil accumulating in their livers and kidneys.

Despite being trained to analyze such devastation through a scientist's eyes, Craig couldn't not have an emotional reaction to the Exxon Valdez oil spill. "That place was so much home to me. I'd worked out there and played out there for almost fifteen years before the spill, so it felt like having someone come into my house and just desecrate it. People who had no sense or knowledge of the area were running the entire show. The place was as close as you can get to a war zone. Everything was out of control. It made me realize the ephemeral nature of things. Things can turn on a dime."

The far-reaching effects of the spill are still unknown, and the goal is to continue the study well into the future. Such long-term research has been made possible with settlement money from the oil company; the funds are paid as an endowment with a significant portion set aside for research. Craig explained, "This study is still one of the backbones of what we do that keeps research consistently anchored and provides an opportunity to study other aspects of killer whale ecology as well."

Another active research project that the North Gulf Oceanic Society manages under the leadership of Kim Parsons is in regard to killer whale genetics across the North Pacific. Craig and his colleagues have established a detailed picture of the numerous separate populations of killer whales across the North Pacific. In addition, the genetics of the killer whale prey are examined. "I'm working with the salmon genetics lab in Nanaimo, British Columbia, to see what stocks of salmon are most important to the Resident, fish-eating killer whales," Craig said. "Now, we can take a sample when a whale kills a fish and determine what river the fish came from, which helps us to know which rivers are really important to these whales."

He has also been involved in a genetics study on Beluga whales in Alaska. Populations of genetically unique populations of belugas in Cook Inlet and Kotzebue Sound have declined, perhaps beyond recovery. "Subsistence hunting was too much for them, and they're not coming back at the moment," Craig said.

Craig explained that when a population gets knocked down enough, even if predation stops, it often isn't possible for it to recover. This predicament is known as the Allee effect: a reduction in population size negatively impacts an individual's fitness and ability to survive, limiting the capacity of that population to overcome additional threats (such as diseases and climate change).

Oil spills aren't the only chemical pollution threat to marine life. "PCBs have been an issue too," Craig declared. PCBs, or polychlorinated biphenyls, are human-produced toxins released into the marine environment through industrial and agricultural runoff and atmospheric transport (via rainfall, snow, or fog). Although commercial production of PCBs (which were used widely in electrical equipment beginning in 1929) was banned by the Environmental Protection Agency because of the effects on human health, the contaminants are still present in many pre-1979 products.

PCBs are considered "persistent organic pollutants." Once they are in the environment, they bind strongly to soil and sediment and can be transported long distances. In the marine environment, they build up within the fatty tissues of marine organisms. Since killer whales are at the top of the food chain, they have an extremely high concentration of PCBs in their tissues, which affects their ability to reproduce and increases their susceptibility to cancer and other diseases. Although PCBs have been banned, household flame retardants—which are thought to produce a similar effect—are still manufactured, and their use is on the rise.

One aspect of human behavior that Craig believes is headed in the right direction for marine mammals is the whale watching industry. "Whale watching offers the opportunity to bring people into closer contact with the animals in a way that gives them an appreciation for them," he shared. "Around one hundred thousand people go through Kenai, Alaska, on tour boats every year, and probably around twenty thousand to thirty thousand through Prince William Sound."

There is a "negative and positive side to the balance sheet," Craig pointed out. Such an abundance of visitors—and therefore boats on the water—can negatively influence the natural behaviors of marine mammals by creating noise pollution and a plethora of obstacles to avoid in the water. However, Craig is inspired by boat regulations that have been put into place since he started his research work.

For example, vessels are not to approach whales within one hundred yards, are not to be placed in the path of oncoming whales, and are to operate at a slow, safe speed when near whales. In addition, voluntary codes of conduct are in place through a program called Whale SENSE Alaska; businesses that successfully complete a training and evaluation are identified by the Whale SENSE logo. Customers can therefore actively seek out and support responsible whale watching companies.

One component of the program is the commitment to educating naturalists, captains, and passengers. Therefore, whale watching trips are used as a platform for education, not just entertainment; visitors are encouraged to engage in ocean stewardship. Craig considers these improvements reward for so many years spent conducting research and attempting to educate the public. "It's nice to realize that the attention our work brought to the whales out there does change things a bit."

Much of the work he did "out there" was with his research and life partner, Eva Saulitis. The couple worked together for eleven years—she was his graduate student—before their union turned romantic. In total, their research partnership spanned thirty-one years. "We fought like crazy those first years." He smiled. "She was as stubborn as I am." He clarified that their disagreements were respectful, however. "We weren't always in agreement, but we were always on the same track. We had an obvious connection, and that gave us so much juice to be able to do the research we did."

Some of their journey together is outlined in Eva's book, *Into Great Silence*, which chronicles the sudden and subsequently gradual decline of the population of orcas most affected by the Exxon Valdez oil spill—and was written while she experienced her own health deteriorate as cancer took over her body. Eva's passing in 2016 served as a catalyst for Craig's readiness to embark in a new direction himself. "I feel it's time to explore other things, to do more inward work," he shared.

Much of the advice he has to offer young people interested in pursuing a career in his field pertains to doing more inward work, as well. Over the course of his career, he has been frequently approached by young people asking, "How can I get out on your boat?" They feel a connection to the whales and feel that field research is the way to express that passion. But before Craig encourages them to pursue that path, he wants them to dig deeper.

"Try to understand what really motivates you. Is it something out of your mind or out of your heart?" he asks them. "People can get transfixed about having to do something that's 'on their list,' but the one really big lesson I have for young people is to be ready to take some U-turns and right turns and left turns. Just because you want something doesn't mean you will make it happen," he stated.

"In this country, it is reinforced that if you just work hard, you'll get what you want. But there's more to it than that. There's also paying attention to if that path is opening up for you, or if you're being pushed in another direction. Are you being embraced by what you're doing? Are things opening up to make that goal happen for you? That's when you know you're on the right path. If not, you're probably meant to be on another track, and that's OK."

Craig shared that, a number of times, students who want to get out on his research boat don't really understand what they're asking for. "I had a couple of graduate students who were so pumped on whales; they'd seen them briefly on tour boats, so they thought they wanted to get out there and do fieldwork. But, like a lot of people, they didn't realize how seasick you can get on small boats. It's not for everybody."

He added that, when you're out for two weeks at a time on a small boat with people who aren't your closest friends, it's not as pleasant as one might think. "And you can go days without seeing anything—or when you do see whales, they're not doing what you want them to do. You have to be extremely patient." He explained that if the student is used to studying land animals—whose behaviors are about 80 percent observable—it can be frustrating to attempt to observe marine mammals, whose behaviors are only 20 percent observable, or less.

When considering who to accept onto his boat, what makes a graduate student stand out to Craig is when that person asks what can be done to prepare for field research. "That's when I start to pay more interest. I tell them that it's an academic endeavor, so it involves a lot of studying, raising money, and a whole lot of dirty work. Field research is a lot more than just studying animals," he emphasized.

"Most people are not aware of what it's like to have to sit out on the boat for the length of time needed to do what we do. It's a lifestyle. You have to be willing to spend significant time in situations that aren't that comfortable. It sounds great, but so many people come out and are over it pretty fast." He laughed. "What do you really want to do this for?" he makes a point to ask. "You need to come in with more than just wanting to be out on the boat seeing whales."

However, if students are certain "that this is what they have to be doing for no logical reason," Craig will give further advice as to how to prepare for the job. "Nowadays, there's a huge technological piece to this work, such as the use of drones. Then there's acoustic studies, which involves putting out remote recorders and conducting lab analysis. You're going to have to be technologically more advanced than me. In the beginning, I just had to know how to work a camera well."

For younger generations, possessing technological skills may not be the most challenging factor—instead, what Craig considers harder to come by for young people is practical knowledge. "It's necessary for young people to get away from electronic devices at times and realize they need to be able to figure out why something is breaking—especially with the equipment we use on the boat. You need to be able to turn a wrench. People will look at you a lot differently if you have small-boat and mechanical experience and knowledge and not just know how to run a computer really well."

Beyond advances in technology, the field of marine biology was in a very different place when Craig entered the scene. "There was so little known forty-some years ago when I started. There were probably only five guys in the country doing work on cetaceans in particular, and most of it was captive work." One of those pioneering men was Craig's professor, Ken Norris, who served as an early mentor and motivator for Craig's budding career.

He shared, "Ken taught me to go out in the world and look carefully. I always loved animals, but he taught me how to be with animals and really pay attention." There was so much unknown about cetaceans at the time that it didn't take much observation to discover something new. "Now, it's different. You have to use new technology, and it's a bit more tedious than it was to make these 'gee whiz' type of breakthroughs."

He clarified that there is still so much to learn—"we really know nothing"—but the techniques required to discover new information are more complex. "If you don't have a new way of getting in there in some way and looking at the animals, it's a little hard to get support." At the same time, there's a lot more competition for funding than when he started out.

When asked what some of his career highlights have been, he had many to share—none of which were the high-profile speaking gigs or TV shows he's been featured on, but rather experiences he's had in the field. One that stands out was in the shallow waters near False Pass, Alaska, when transient whales were attacking and killing gray whales. It's a scene that can be hard to watch, but since it is a display that comes from a survival instinct within a natural system, it's not nearly as painful as witnessing death caused by some human behaviors.

"There were birds eating the bits and pieces of the whales that washed up; there were brown bears and wolves scavenging carcasses on the beach and sharks taking chunks out of sunken carcasses. It was so raw, so dramatic. That was the most unbelievable time I've ever spent in the field."

Another suprising experience for Craig was witnessing the dichotomy of humpback whale behaviors. "Humpbacks can be more aggressive with each other than killer whales, but they can also be incredibly docile. Here in Hawaii there are groups of males that violently charge after each other; they ram into each other and have blood on the nobs on their snouts. But then there are also the males who are singers, and those animals are often solitary and very gentle." He was even lucky enough to witness what may be courting behavior. "Seeing very quiet, sedate pairs of animals do their own little ballet in an incredibly gentle way was one of the most beautiful underwater scenes I've witnessed."

Witnessing nature do what nature does is what gives Craig reason to be hopeful about the future. Despite having been witness to one of the most catastrophic man-made, seaside disasters in history, he believes that the universe operates via natural stages of openings and contractions. "The times when there are incredible contractions is when there has to be an increase in education and awareness." With the latter, he explained, come more openings.

"There are forces at play here we don't understand, and we never will—or at least not in my lifetime. But if you look back to the dark ages and then Renaissance period and what's happening now with consciousness, there have been openings and closings all along. And right now, there is a bigger opening than ever before. And I'm not an optimist." He laughed. "It's something deeper. It's a deeper sense of what is."

To learn more about the North Gulf Oceanic Society, visit www.whalesalaska.org.

VI
THE WEB OF LIFE

Not only cetaceans face the threat of extinction in this web of life—a critical food source for orcas, bears, eagles, and also many Indigenous peoples is also endangered. That food source is salmon. The lack of salmon is perhaps foremost responsible for the faltering population of Southern Resident killer whales, though 137 species in the Northwest alone depend on the presence of salmon.

Salmon is a species that has survived 10 million years of volcanic eruptions, earthquakes, glacial advances, and geomagnetic reversals. It is a tragic fault of our species that it has taken only a few centuries of Euro-American settlement to nearly wipe out what had thus far been so remarkably resilient. Even in 1875, it was well-known that the collapse of Atlantic salmon fisheries was due to lack of both fishing regulations and habitat protection, but Pacific Northwest communities would nonetheless choose to follow the same practices.

As recently as the early twentieth century, it was common for a fisherman to haul home Chinook salmon that weighed over one hundred pounds each. Today, it is a shocking occurrence to find a thirty-pound salmon. For the Southern Resident orcas that evolved to eat a diet primarily based on hundred-pound salmon, that means a lot more hunting is required in order to meet their daily dietary requirements.

Hunting becomes significantly more challenging when fish stocks are smaller and fewer, and noise in the water (due to an abundance of boats) is far greater than ever before. The lack of sufficient food causes this population of orcas to experience a miscarriage rate of 69 percent (which can kill the pregnant mother too). Half of all newborn calves who manage to be born alive die within their first year of life. This high mortality rate is the result of poisonous toxins in the mother's body. When the animals are not

finding enough to eat, their bodies begin burning fat reserves—
which house toxins from the polluted waters in which they swim.

Fish Farms

Overfishing and habitat destruction has led to the decline of wild
fish, but the human appetite for fish did not weaken with it. Salmon
farming began in British Columbia in the early 1970s and the
country currently operates an average of eighty-five net-cage fish
farms. Additional cold-water coastal areas caught on to the trend;
Norway is by far the largest producer of farmed Atlantic salmon in
the world, followed by Chile and the United Kingdom. In the United
States, Washington State operates eight Atlantic salmon net-pen
fish farms (although legislation intends to phase out Atlantic
salmon net-pet farms by the year 2025).

Atlantic salmon are popularly farmed in the Pacific Northwest,
due to its more domesticated nature. They grow faster than Pacific
salmon and don't display aggression while cramped in net pens. It
is supposed that Atlantic salmon can't breed with Pacific salmon,
making that choice seemingly more environmentally sound should
an escape occur.

However, fish farms pose many threats to wild fish and the
entire marine environment. Farmed salmon are bred artificially in
freshwater hatchery vats and then moved to saltwater pens after
eight months. They are raised in nylon net cages open to coastal
waters until they reach market size. In their rearing process, they
are fed pellets of fish meal (ground fish) mixed with fish oil and
byproducts of slaughterhouses including blood meal, ground
chicken feathers, soybeans, poultry meal, and vitamins and
minerals. These pellets are infused with antibiotics, making farmed
fish the most drugged livestock on either land or water.
Additionally, they are dyed pink to appear to consumers like "real"
salmon (wild salmon are naturally pink due to their diet of
zooplankton).

Not only does that diet make for a very unhealthy fish, the
chemicals and toxins released in their feces make for very

unhealthy waters. Prone to disease and parasites, these fish are likely to spread their ailments to other wild fish in the area—such as the thousands of herring and other smaller fish that get stuck in their nets—and thus enter the marine food chain. As if these fish weren't polluted enough, toxic paint is used in the nets that leaches into the fish and into the ocean.

It's hard to believe that there is a commercial demand for these fish. Rather, there is a lack of awareness and education as to just how unhealthy these fish are for human consumption—and even animal consumption. Though not intended to enter the marine environment outside of their pens, accidents do happen—more frequently and dramatically than the industry would have the public believe. The collapse of a pen in Washington in August of 2017 released over three hundred thousand Atlantic salmon into the Salish Sea—making it inevitable that their diseases be passed on to the wild and hatchery-bred salmon that Resident orcas eat.

Hatcheries

There is a lot of controversy around the use of fish hatcheries to supplement declining wild salmon runs. They are not nearly as detrimental to the environment or to the fish themselves as fish farms, although there are concerns that hatcheries can't reproduce the necessary survival instincts and reproductive success that wild salmon have developed over millions of years of evolution.

At hatcheries, fish are artificially bred, hatched, and reared during their early life stages before being released into the wild. Tagging studies reveal that over 75 percent of the salmon caught in Puget Sound waters and 90 percent of the fish caught in the Columbia River are hatchery-raised fish. They do interbreed with wild salmon, which is what tends to make the practice controversial—are hatchery fish diluting the survival skills of wild fish and therefore contributing to the decline in the wild salmon population?

The impact of hatchery fish on wild salmon runs is yet unknown; however, what is known is that hatcheries treat symptoms, not causes. The reasons for the decline in wild salmon runs need to be addressed along with the implementation of hatcheries. Despite the largest wildlife restoration effort in world history (and the investment of $15 billion since 1978), wild salmon from the Columbia River have not recovered enough to be taken off the endangered species list.

Perhaps more critical than recovering endangered wild runs are preserving those few remaining runs that are doing well. The Wild Salmon Center based in Portland, Oregon, is focused on that issue. As a result of their efforts, half the rivers out of Tillamook State Forest are now set aside for wild fish—creating the biggest network of wild fish rivers south of Canada.

These efforts are made even more critical because salmon are considered a "keystone species," or a species on which many other species depend. If they are removed, it would mean a drastic change in the ecosystem, if not total collapse. Without salmon to keep populations of orcas, bears, river otters, birds, and even reptiles and amphibians in balance, new and possibly invasive species would be allowed to populate the habitat.

Dams

There are other critical efforts being made to help ensure the survival of wild and hatchery-bred salmon—and therefore the Southern Resident orcas and others that depend on them for food. Dams present one of the biggest challenges for salmon trying to reach their spawning grounds. Turbines and spillways maul migrating juveniles that were not trapped and hauled around the dam.

Those who manage to successfully maneuver through the maze face predator and pathogen challenges ahead. Their migration is extended from a few days to weeks as they pass through multiple reservoirs. Many fish get lost, sick, stuck in culverts, or feasted upon by birds and sea lions who have found easy targets around the dams. In addition, dams raise the temperature of water— making the waters inhospitable for juvenile salmon.

Hydroelectric power has been marketed as a cleaner source of energy than power plants running on fossil fuels, but in addition to giving off carbon dioxide, dams also give off methane—which is eighty-five times more potent than carbon dioxide. This process occurs as a result of organic material (vegetation, sediment, and soil) that flows from rivers into reservoirs and decomposes, polluting the water and then the air. Studies indicate that in places where organic material is the highest, dams can actually contribute more greenhouse gases into the air than coal-fired powerplants.

Yet the United States alone operates an estimated eighty-four thousand dams, impounding six hundred thousand miles of river, or 17 percent of the country's rivers. Of these dams, many are aging and in need of repair or removal—some of these are "deadbeat dams," or dams that are no longer productive. With an average lifespan of only fifty years, 85 percent of them will need expensive repairs by the year 2020. Many of them are certainly not worth the investment, but tearing them down is a drawn-out, bureaucratic process.

Some campaigns have made it through that process, however. The largest dam removal in US history was that of the Washington State Elwha Dam in 2012, followed by the Glines Canyon Dam in 2014. As a result, there has been a steady and remarkable increase in salmon runs. It is a significant move in a positive direction toward freeing more rivers and replenishing food sources for the orcas; however, the recovery effort won't affect whale diets for at least twenty years. All the more reason to take these actions now.

The dam removal projects foremost in the spotlight are the four Lower Snake River dams in southeast Washington State. These dams provide only a tiny fraction of electricity and irrigation to the region; their allowance of goods to be barged downriver could easily be replaced by road or rail. The removal of these dams—and others—would allow salmon to return, and they would allow natural floodwaters to provide seasonal habitat and soil fertilization to the lands and make groundwater recharge possible for badly depleted aquifers.

Logging

It is impossible to talk about the recovery of the Resident orca populations without talking about salmon, and it's impossible to talk about the health of salmon without talking about Northwest forests. For any given year, the bigger the salmon run, the wider the growth ring on trees—indicating the extent to which nutrient-bearing salmon brought from sea to shore fertilize the soil and allow for increased tree growth.

When Northwest forests are clear-cut (a logging practice where most if not all trees in an area are cut down at the same time), the private logging companies and state and federal entities that own them try to speed the regrowth process by spraying herbicides on all natural pioneer species in order to make room for the cash cow: genetically modified, uniformly planted Douglas Fir trees. These trees are tall and fast-growing, but it takes years before they can offer the shade necessary to maintain the natural and cooler water temperatures in which salmon can survive. Additionally, the herbicides used in the process enter the rivers and can be lethal to fish.

Do not be fooled by replanting propaganda. For example, although Oregon has stricter reforestation laws than most states, the method in which landowners (including the state) are required to regrow logged forests is not a sustainable method that supports a diverse ecosystem. In a healthy process, only a small portion of a forest would be cut down at a time and allowed to grow back naturally. This would mean leafy deciduous trees would spring forth first, followed by bushes. These plants grow quickly and manage water temperatures by offering shade to streams.

The roots of these trees would prevent erosion and the creation of a gravel surface that can't hold and incubate salmon eggs. With time, young evergreen and conifer trees would appear, feeding on the decomposition of their predecessor's leaves and further aiding in the control of water temperatures.

Perhaps we should take our cues from nature, which makes sure that not all organisms in an area are the same. If a virus or bacteria breaks out, all members of a single species are doomed. Diversity ensures the survival of plants and trees and all life forms that depend on them—including, in the end, ourselves.

LYLA SNOVER: *Witnessing Change*

Visiting with Lyla Snover is like gaining access to a living history of Whidbey Island: the land, the people, and the wildlife. Through her eighty-four years of memories and observations, she's able to shine a unique light on what needs to be paid attention to. In some ways, her observations offer hope; she has witnessed a stark change in attitudes and behaviors regarding people's relationships with animals, the earth, and the water. She has also noticed a significant reduction in fish—and fewer orca sightings.

Part of the latter is the result of the Penn Cove captures in August of 1970—when orcas were driven into the cove through the use of explosives and helicopters in order to display the younger whales at marine parks. But it's also the repercussions of overfishing and the pollution of Salish Sea waters. What Lyla saw that fateful day at Penn Cove—and over the years from her island home—served as the catalyst for an abundance of future stewardship.

Lyla is a "Coupeville girl." She is a fifth-generation Whidbey Island resident—a descendant of one of five pioneer families who came to the island in the 1850s and 1860s. She has seen the population of her town go from 350 people at the time of her high school graduation in 1952 to nearly 2,000 people in 2017.

Whales were a part of her childhood. She recalls her grandmother sharing stories of rowing a boat among pods of orcas. Her grandmother told her, "People call them killer whales, but they won't hurt you. They don't bother anybody." She also remembers going fishing with her father near Fort Casey, where they'd see the same gray whale every year. "He'd just roll around out there. I called him Oscar." Lyla laughed. "Only when he came up between the boat and shore was it kind of spooky. He was a lot bigger than our boat."

Though the whales may have been amiable to humans, not everyone felt amiable toward the whales. She recalled how when she was young, everyone hunted, so everyone had guns. She would see people standing out on the bluff, shooting at what was in the water—which would sometimes be orcas or porpoises. "To think about it now, it really makes your heart hurt," Lyla lamented. "But that's just the way it was in those days. They didn't think about what they were doing or that the orcas might be endangered sometime."

For Lyla, the whales provided less a source of entertainment, more a sense of awe. "Seeing them while out fishing on the boat was one thing, but to see them here in the cove was really impressive." She recalled having had a picnic on the beach one day when a pod of orcas came within one hundred feet of the beach. "There were probably eight of them, and they were spyhopping and playing around for about an hour. I loved that. To have them here where I live is really precious." Lyla paused before adding, "I wish they'd come back more often."

She knows why they do not. She was witness to the August 8, 1970, capture. Her memories of the event are more about what she heard than what she saw. "I could only look twice, for very short times, because it was so sad. The vocalizing is what I remember the most. It sounded like they were crying, and it would just bring tears to my eyes."

She remembers seeing smaller whales being separated from the larger whales. The sounds they were making still haunt her. "I had never heard them make sounds before; I didn't know they could. It was an eerie sound. I couldn't stand to listen to them. It just didn't feel right." She was with her sister and her sister's two young children at the time. The children were asking, "Why are they doing that? Why don't they let them go?" They knew it was wrong too.

When Lyla spoke next, her words appeared to be an afterthought, but more likely they were a memory intentionally kept buried that suddenly rose to the surface. "Another thing about when they captured them...I was out at the grocery store, and a truck went by with a big orca on the flatbed. I don't know if it was dead or alive. I know they buried at least one orca that died at the old garbage dump, and it could have been that one. Or they could have been transporting a live one to an aquarium. Either way, it was shocking. It was not a good picture."

Those disturbing images and sounds from the capture sparked a passion in Lyla to learn what she could about the magnificent animals. "Since that capture, everyone I know who saw them feels kind of like I do; they're such big, beautiful animals. People fell more in love with them and became more aware of how special they are. Orcas, especially—a gray whale is gorgeous, but it doesn't have the same beauty as an orca. If you see them, you can't help but be impressed."

Lyla's first entry into island stewardship was to join what was then known as Beach Watchers. Currently known as Sound Water Stewards of Island County, the program began as an extension of Washington State University but now is an independent nonprofit organization. The program consists of one hundred hours of classroom and hands-on training. Instructors are brought in from various backgrounds and emphases to teach participants about everything from soils, septic tanks, and composting to whales, vertebrates, and beach ecology. After graduation, participants commit to fifty hours of volunteer community outreach for two consecutive years.

The latter was a requirement Lyla dove into with enthusiasm. "I gave talks in schools, talks on the ferry...anywhere and anytime I could get three people together." The emphasis of her talks was water quality because "you can't live without water, and you don't get new water—it just recycles." She did a demonstration about pollutants in the water: "I took a nice clean bottle of water and then added sugar and oil and molasses to represent pesticides and pollutants. Then I'd say, 'I don't want to swim around in this water. I don't want to drink this water.' And then I'd drink some. The kids were in awe. They'd say, 'Is that really dog poop in there?'"

Lyla's involvement with Beach Watchers did not stop there. In December of 1998, the body of a starving gray whale washed up on

Whidbey Island. Dead whales washed ashore on the island are considered the responsibility of the property owners to dispose of. People have used dynamite or chainsaws in an attempt to break the bodies down, while others have tried to bury them or tow them out to sea. (A somewhat amusing case is that of a dead sperm whale that washed up on an Oregon beach in 1970. In an attempt to rid the beach of the decomposing corpse, twenty cases of dynamite—instead of twenty sticks—were used. Onlookers and cars were covered in whale particles.)

With this particular gray whale, which was named Rosie, forty Beach Watchers volunteers decided to wade into the shallows and spend four days removing blubber and entrails in an effort to salvage the thirty-two-foot-long skeleton for educational purposes. Lyla was among them.

"That was a stinky job," she recalled. "When they first found it and decided to deflesh it, I already had a vacation in Mexico planned, so I had to leave." She smiled at her great fortune. "I didn't have to take all the rotten flesh and cut it up, but I helped clean the skeleton and scrape it and put it back together. Then we painted it with Elmer's glue and white paint to make it solid and clean."

Lyla had never imagined the amount of work that would go into such a task. It took two years and a great many volunteers to complete the project. Still, she considered the job "an interesting and fun thing to do." The skeleton currently hangs at the Coupeville, Washington, wharf and is still called Rosie, even though he was later discovered to be male.

Of course, Lyla prefers opportunities to comingle with live whales, rather than dead ones. Several years ago, she took advantage of an opportunity to visit the gray whale birthing lagoons in Baja California, Mexico, on a trip led by Orca Network. "We actually got to kiss a gray whale!" Lyla exclaimed with childlike enthusiasm. She described the adventure: "We flew down to San Diego, then took a bus across the border and then a small plane to a lagoon, where we camped for about three days. The boats are about eighteen feet long; they just go out in the lagoon and stop— the whales come to you. And they're bigger than the boat!"

Lyla giggled before continuing, "They come right up and gently touch the boat, and the moms occasionally nudge their babies toward the boat. They're so close that they blow in your face, and it stinks! But that's part of the experience." In Mexico, it is not illegal to touch the whales, as it is in the United States, so long as the whales approach the boats on their own accord. The Mexican government has established strong whale watching guidelines to regulate the industry and promote the conservation of the gray whale species and habitat.

Lyla attempted to describe the ethereal experience of looking into the eye of a whale. "It's almost like a religious experience. It's just awesome. It's like they really *know*. You can see their intelligence. You know they're probably a lot more intelligent than you." She chuckled. "You can't describe it. It's just...precious. You want to do it again. You want to talk to them. I'd like to know what they're thinking and where they've been and what they are doing and what they feel about us." She paused before adding a final line with conviction and passion, "And how we can do *better*."

It didn't take long for Lyla to answer her own question. "Well, more fish." She has personally witnessed the decline of many fish species from her own beach property. "I used to go fishing a lot with my dad. We would go out at five in the morning before school, and we would catch fifteen- or thirty-pound salmon. Now people are lucky if they catch a fish at all. People don't realize how changed it is, how many fewer resources we have."

Lyla remembered how thousands of smelt used to come to her beach and spawn. With nostalgia, she recalled what they used to taste like and how easy they were to catch. "You could just catch them with your hands. They'd come in down by the dock, and people would just go down and wait with a long pole with a wire basket and just scoop them up."

She doesn't know what exactly is responsible for the decline, but she suspects it has something to do with the state having issued permits to bottom-fish in the location years ago. "There would be ten or twelve big commercial fishing boats out dragging across the sea floor for bottom fish. If they took all the eel grass and all the vegetation off the bottom, to me that's probably why the smelt or feeder fish left."

Lyla continued her path down memory lane, "We used to fish off the dock and catch nice perch that we sold for a dime. And bullheads—we caught bullheads by the dozens. And I don't see those fish down there off the dock at all anymore."

She has seen positive shifts in the environment and human behaviors and education, however. "The Dungeness crab are starting to come back, so maybe they will recover if they are left alone. And now, my seven great-grandkids know more about orcas than I ever did at their age. South Whidbey Elementary School has the orca as their mascot. People are learning."

Although none of the people who were involved in the 1970 Penn Cove capture were from Whidbey Island, Lyla is inspired by the number of people locally and worldwide fighting for the release of Lolita—and the change of heart many of the people who worked on the capture have had. "So many of them have stated that they won't do it again and they're sorry they did it."

She has also lived long enough to see the return of some local Indigenous traditions. When she was a child no older than seven, she remembers attending the annual Coupeville Water Festival, which began in the 1930s. The event featured Native American canoe racing and Native foods, entertainment, crafts and culture. Lyla was part of the volunteer community that brought the historic festival back, which was renamed the Penn Cove Water Festival. The event has become another opportunity to educate the public on not just local Indigenous history, but the importance of protecting the area's natural resources.

Lyla has taken everything she's learned through her years of island stewardship and education to heart. She limits her personal water use, understanding that, though rainwater on the island is plentiful, the growth in development on the island relies on aquifers—which can run dry. She recycles and has since "before it was popular." She doesn't buy things with bubble wrap or plastic wrap. She plants trees—practicing that for every tree cut down, one or more should be planted. And she teaches her great-grandchildren how to better protect the environment. "This kind of education is all tied together with whales, the water environment, and pollution. It all fits together," she added.

Becoming so active in environmental issues has offered unexpected, priceless benefits to Lyla's life. She has formed tight bonds with other volunteers, whale lovers, and stewards in the area. She hosts an annual summer gathering, which she has named Camp Run Amok, at her beach property. The group consists of women age fifty-five and up. Lyla is the "matriarch." The group stays at the beach for three or four days and "does all kinds of crazy things." Men are occasionally allowed but under strict guidelines: "They can come down if they bring food or wine, and they can stay ten minutes."

Joking aside, Lyla is grateful for the camaraderie the group has formed and the synergy that has resulted in the community as a result. "We're all interested in the same thing. We all care about what is happening in the community and the world, and that brings us together." It's as though the women have formed their own pod, as orcas do. Perhaps, through the group's combined efforts, orcas may gradually return to the island that now eight generations of Lyla's family have called home.

To learn more about volunteer opportunities and trainings through Sound Water Stewards, visit www.soundwaterstewards.org. *For more information on the Penn Cover Water Festival, visit* www.penncovewaterfestival.com. Photo by Mary Jo Adams.

RAY FRYBERG: *We Are the Vanguard*

Similar to how it's impossible to talk about the recovery of the Southern Resident killer whale population without talking about recovery efforts for salmon, it's not possible to talk about salmon recovery without talking about the necessary resurgence of Indigenous philosophy and practices.

For thousands of years, Native peoples have served as the ultimate stewards of salmon and, therefore, everything that depends on them. Their role of stewardship hasn't changed—it just has become a lot more difficult to practice. Ray Fryberg is at the forefront of efforts to break through bureaucracy and rebuild salmon runs in the Pacific Northwest; he has served as fisheries director and natural and cultural resources director for the Tulalip Tribes for over ten years.

His tribe is a member of the Northwest Indian Fisheries Commission, an organization that was created following the critical 1974 ruling known as the Boldt Decision (for which Ray conducted research as a member of Tulalip's tribal fishery) that established tribal members as natural resource comanagers with the state of Washington. Ray uses his position and his passion to speak for the rights not only of the tribe but of the killer whales who depend on fish and clean waters for survival.

When Ray speaks, it's hard not to listen. His gentle but commanding presence bodes well for the advocacy work he does on behalf of the Northwest tribe he represents. He is not afraid to stand up for what he believes in, and one thing he believes in most of all is the cultural and spiritual importance of the killer whale to his tribe's wellbeing.

The Tulalip Indian Reservation is located forty miles north of Seattle, Washington, and includes sixteen miles of marine shoreline along the Salish Sea—critical habitat for the endangered

Southern Resident killer whales. The tribe therefore shares fishing territory with the whales; for centuries, both the tribe and the whales have relied on salmon to sustain themselves.

That codependent relationship contributes to the place of high honor the killer whale holds for the tribe. It is the symbol of the Tulalip; tribal members are known as killer whale people, or brothers of the killer whale. Ray remembered being told stories about how when his ancestors were traveling on the water and saw killer whales, they would stop and back their canoes in toward the shore. The act was a sign of respect. "If you come into another people's territory, you come in backward, which means you're coming in nonaggressively."

In their oral history, the killer whale is known for having saved the tribe from starvation. "We have watched the whales fish, and we have learned from them," Ray shared. Some of his earliest recollections revolve around learning how to fish in collaboration with the killer whales.

He grew up on the reservation during a time when there were no jobs available to Native peoples other than fishing. At the beginning of the spring salmon season, all families on the reservation worked collectively to fish the coastline. As a child in the early 1950s, Ray used a fishing technique called beach seining— a fishing net was hung vertically in the water with its bottom edge held down by weights and its top edge buoyed by floats. During this busy season, the fishermen would live on the beach to maximize their gains.

Ray offered insight into just how intertwined fishing was with his youth. "Fishing was a family effort that was carried into our culture. The youngest children started out with the smallest job of pulling in the web, and then when they were bigger, they would pull the lead lines in until eventually the family said, 'Get on the boat and make a set.' It was a rite of passage, an introduction into manhood by the time the family felt you had enough skills to skipper the boat."

Fishing served as not only an economic necessity for the tribe but also one of sustenance. Even today, the fish consumption rate of Tulalip members is five times higher than the fish consumption rate of the average American. In the days of Ray's youth, enough fish had to be smoked and canned to sustain his family throughout the winter. A good catch was necessary for their survival.

It was as if the killer whales understood this delicate balance too. Ray recalled how some mornings he would still be in bed when he'd wake to the unmistakable *pffffffff* sound of an orca blow. "We'd hear them before we would see them," he remembered. "Everybody knew that when the killer whales came in they were going to drive the fish in toward the beach." The sound activated the fishermen. "Everyone would make a quick set right out on the beach in front of the whales."

Many years ago, an elder taught Ray that by watching the killer whale he could tell what the salmon were going to do. Sure enough, salmon would inevitably come to shore while fleeing the killer whales and easily get caught in their nets. After the initial frenzy, the fishermen also knew that the salmon were going to disappear for a while. "A lot of times people would just stop fishing for a day or two once the killer whales went through because they alarmed the fish so much," Ray remembered.

As Ray got older, the fishing technique used changed to gill netting, which was done deeper out. He remembered being out at Salmon Bank off the San Juan Islands (the archipelago of islands off the state of Washington that includes San Juan Island) when killer whales swam by. "I could tell they were fishing because they were slapping their fins, which is how they drive fish. So, I raced ahead in my boat and set net out in the deep area in front of the killer whales so when they came off the shallow part and swam in, they naturally herded fish into my net. I caught around eight hundred fish that morning, when everyone else was catching much smaller numbers." It pays to pay attention to where the whales are.

Or at least, it used to. Fish aren't nearly as abundant as they used to be, and Ray is deeply concerned that the killer whales are not getting enough to eat. The tribe's responsibility to the killer whale is one he takes seriously. "We need to do our part to protect them," he shared. "I consider them a barometer of what's going on out there in the water, because our diets are very similar." When addressing the tribal fishery's salmon allocation, an allocation for the killer whales is also considered.

He explained, "All of the commercial and tribal fisheries are allowed a certain amount of impact on salmon runs, according to the river of origin. It all gets divided up. At the Fraser River, for example, we are allowed an incidental catch of Chinook, which is the primary food source for the killer whales. After we get to that number, we can no longer sell them commercially because the remaining portion is to be set aside for the killer whales."

Ray added that, when determining allotments, another aspect of consideration should be those marine mammals who consume salmon as their choice diet. He shared, "We spend a lot of money and effort to restore habitat and salmon runs but in order to do so we need to have the seals and sea lions be part of the equation because they are eating a lot of our efforts—around fifty percent of our stock."

Although fish allotment is a piece of the puzzle, Ray understands there is a much larger picture that needs to be considered. The main food source for the Southern Resident killer whales is Columbia River Chinook salmon, which rear themselves among the San Juan Islands. Lack of production out of the Columbia River due to the impact of dams is a much bigger issue, he believes, than allotment. "If you're really going to do something for the killer whales, you need to find out what is really affecting them and make the right adjustments."

He feels particularly passionate about voicing his views on the impact fish hatcheries have on wild salmon runs. Anti-hatchery groups recently filed a lawsuit against the state of Washington, placing the Snohomish, Skagit, and Nooksack River hatcheries under review. "Our hatcheries are in the spotlight right now as part of that review, but eventually that review is going to affect the over 150 hatcheries in the state," he shared. "We love native salmon, but the effect of hatcheries is not the issue of their survival. The decline of wild salmon was marked a long time ago, before there were hatcheries. Hatcheries were put in place to try to help the salmon runs."

Numerous issues are responsible for the salmon run declines. Several quickly and easily rolled off his tongue: global warming, development, population increase, ocean acidification, agriculture, lack of biofilters, lower river levels, higher river temperatures, groundwater contamination. "Those are the big-picture issues," he stated. "Hatcheries have only a small impact."

Ray believes it's time to "hit the reset button" and start evaluating the potential for wild salmon stocks to rebuild—taking into account all aspects of the equation—and then "let science speak for itself." He added that Chinook salmon have not been commercially fished in the tribe's river system for over thirty years. "We thought that by taking even four years of commercial pressure off of them they would start to rebuild." Unfortunately, they have only continued to decline. "Even if we introduce more fish into the habitat, the habitat can't handle that increase."

He regrets that there are no funds set aside for federal or state enforcement of environmental protection for salmon habitat. "The tribes are it. We are the vanguard," he declared. "We do a lot to try and keep the salmon runs going—not just for us, but for everybody—but we all have to work together." He described how there are so many departments involved in the issue—NOAA, the Northwest Fisheries Commission, the Department of Justice, the Department of Interior—each with its own guidelines, that it's extremely difficult to make any progress.

"All of our efforts have to move in the same direction. If we want to make a difference, we have to work as hard at preservation and production as we do fighting each other. Then we'll start to get somewhere." He added, "Instead of fighting over protecting the fish, we're fighting over the last few fish."

Despite that bleak assessment, Ray does feel positive movement. "We've crossed bridges and have made alliances. People do realize that the work we do is really beneficial." Part of the work Ray does is visit schools and give educational talks. He tries to teach the students to be careful what they put in the ground and in the water, because it all ends up in the ocean and affects the fish and the whales. When he's speaking to high school students, he encourages them to go on to study environmental science. "You can work for any tribe in the country, forestry, fisheries, hunting, and so forth. Environmental fields are where the jobs are now."

He believes careers in the field will be abundant due to the effects of climate change, which he considers one of the most critical issues affecting the Pacific Northwest and beyond. "The city of Seattle is going to have to adjust to sea level rise. As the temperature increases, water volume increases. Puget Sound is going to rise two feet by the end of this century. Seattle is right at water level, so that swell is going to push water back to the eastern side of the city. That requires some major overhaul to be able to adjust to that change."

Accelerating climate change is the Canadian government's approval of an expansion of the Kinder Morgan oil pipeline, which poses a critical threat to salmon habitat and the killer whale's diet in addition to the waters the killer whales frequent. The expansion, if not derailed by opponents and activists, will increase oil tanker traffic through the Salish Sea from five tankers per month to thirty-four tankers per month. Each of those vessels carries with it the risk of an accident and the release of fuel.

Ray recently spoke in court on behalf of the tribe in regard to the Coast Guard's failure to consult with the National Marine Fisheries Service on the increase in vessel traffic. He pointed out that the Exxon Valdez oil spill essentially wiped out an entire population of genetically unique Transient orcas that were swimming in nearby waters. A large oil spill would be catastrophic for the already-endangered Southern Resident killer whales, the fisheries, and all organisms (including humans) who rely on a habitable Salish Sea for their survival. It's a position he defends often.

Ray said, "Whenever we do treaty protection, I always break the issue down into our spiritual and cultural connection to salmon and the killer whales, which are the fabric of our culture and who we are as a people. We wear clothes like everybody else and live in houses and drive cars and have an education, but we're still Indian people. We still have our beliefs, and we're still really connected to the earth the land and the water and everything that surrounds us."

Efforts to assimilate Tulalip members through colonization and the outlawing of their culture, language, songs, and dances have taken place in Western Washington since the advancement of the first settlers. A government-run boarding school opened near the Tulalip reservation in 1857 and remained open until 1932, which sought to isolate Native children from their families and traditions and instead "educate" them in the ways of the newly dominant American culture.

"That really turned our culture upside down. It had some real negative effects on us." Ray explained how those historical traumas led many Native people to self-medicate through the use of drugs or alcohol. He shared that the tribe is working to reverse that damage, but in order to find healing, it needs to reclaim its own culture. "We need to rediscover our self-identity and learn to have self-esteem again," he shared. "We need to remember that we were made and put here by the creator, and that the creator doesn't make any mistakes."

One piece of the puzzle required to rebuild their culture is to reconnect with the symbol of their tribe—the killer whale. Ray had the opportunity to engage with the spirit of the killer whale in a meaningful way while canoeing in Nootka Sound off Vancouver Island in 2004. He had lost his brother in 2003 on a canoe journey (a traditional event where Native tribes travel by ocean-going canoe with their families to a host destination where songs and dances are shared). The loss deeply affected Ray; the two had grown close while his brother built canoes on which Ray taught paddle songs to Native youth in an effort to restore part of the tribe's culture and traditions.

While on a canoe journey the year following his brother's passing, Ray encountered Mowachaht First Nations people who told him the story of one of their chiefs who had said he was going to die soon but that he'd come back to life as a killer whale. A week after the chief's death in 2001, a killer whale showed up near their land and had been hanging out in the area ever since. Ray was deeply intrigued by the story due to his tribe's connection to the killer whale; he shared his interest in meeting the whale with the Mowachaht people, and he and his family were invited to come back after the journey to be introduced.

"I loaded up my canoe and had several members of my family with me: my daughters, my son, my grandchildren, my mother-in-law and sister-in-law and my niece. There were seventeen of us," he began the story. "We took my canoe up there to Gold River and met up with the Mowachaht tribe. They said, 'He usually hangs out by this rock,' so we paddled out there, and we didn't see him. After two or three hours, we thought, 'Well, we gave it our best shot.' We started paddling back in as the wind picked up off the ocean. We got up on some of those waves and surfed back in real fast. Just as we got back to the dock, a lady on shore said her uncle and his family had called from their canoe; they were with the killer whale out at the rock. They asked, 'What do you want to do, Ray?' I said, 'I've come a long way. Let's go back out there.'"

Ray and his family paddled back out on the ocean, and sure enough, there he was—the killer whale, known among Native peoples as Tsu'xiit, swimming near the other family's canoe. They began singing the paddle song of the chief who had passed away and claimed he would return as a killer whale. Ray remembered, "He heard that song and stopped for a second before turning toward us and coming at us on the surface like a torpedo. The water was shooting over the top of his head, and then he went down and then popped up and blew. The blow startled me—it was really powerful. Then he popped his head up out of the water alongside me and looked me right in the eye. We never took our eyes off of each other. I knew that we were examining each other. It felt like he knew something that I didn't."

The whale was introduced to Ray by the Mowachaht tribal members in their language. Tsu'xiit was told, "This is Ray Fryberg and his whole family. They came all the way from Washington to meet you and pay their respects. They are like our family; we've adopted each other, and we travel on our canoes together, and our families sing and dance together."

Then Ray introduced himself to the whale by his Native name. Tsu'xiit held Ray's gaze the whole time, until he swam forward and went right between the two canoes with his dorsal fin slicing the water, before swimming up in front of Ray's canoe. He got underneath the bow and raised the canoe on the tip of his nose a few feet in the air. "My daughter started to panic, and I said, 'We're OK; he's not going to bother us.'" Then the whale put the canoe back down and swam around it, before lying upside down underneath the canoe with his pectoral fins on either side of it, rubbing the canoe. Ray felt that Tsu'xiit was blessing his family.

Just before the whale swam back up to the surface, a big bubble erupted from his blowhole. Ray was leaning over the canoe and was hit in the face with the whale's breath. "I shared the breath of a killer whale," Ray stated in awe.

But the magic of the experience wasn't over. "He let out a real loud, low, clicking noise. He kept doing that, and then he stopped and rolled over and was looking at me with his mouth open. He started vocalizing real loudly; it sounded like *eee eee eee eee eee*."

Ray later learned from Ken Balcomb at the Center for Whale Research that what Tsu'xiit was doing by clicking was examining Ray's body. "Killer whales are so sophisticated that they can measure your emotional content and tell a lot about whatever is going through you," Ray said. "When he rolled over and started to vocalize, Ken said he was talking to me with his own language and method of communication." After a moment of silence, he completed his story. "We really did connect while we were there."

Because of the recent loss of Ray's brother, the experience held extra meaning for him. He felt as though he'd reconnected with his brother's spirit in a way. The whale had repeatedly pushed Ray's paddle, which his brother had made for him, out of the water, balancing it on his rostrum (forehead). "When he was pushing my paddle, he was looking at me as if to say, 'See this paddle? I made it.' That's what it felt like to me."

After the families returned to the village, they shared an evening of song and dance. The other chief asked Ray, "What was that like for you?" Ray answered, "It was the most powerful spiritual experience I've ever had in my life." He continued, "I've been a hunter and a fisherman pretty much all of my life. I've seen a lot of animals—deer, elk, bears, cougars, all kinds. But I've never, ever been looked at like that killer whale looked at me. There was a sentient *being* in there."

For a culture that had nearly been stripped of the spirituality central to its core, reconnecting with the spirit of a wild animal served as a reminder to Ray of the spirit that resides in all things. "The boarding schools demonized our spirituality; they taught us that our practices are bad and evil. If you hear that long enough, some people actually start to believe it.

"It's true—the legends and stories of my ancestors kind of sound fantastical, but having had an experience with a wild killer whale really validates my belief that my ancestors had those experiences too, and there was some truth to those legends. They were connected to the spirit of all things, and there was nothing wrong with that."

Ray recognized the importance of sharing that message with Native youth—starting with his grandchildren. "I was watching my little grandson—he was two or three at the time—at the edge of the canoe. When that killer whale came up in front and they were nose to nose, that little boy was not afraid. He put his hands up on top of the whale's head and was stroking him, holding him. He pulled his hands off and had water from the killer whale on his hands, and he brushed his hair with it. One day that little boy is going to be sitting around as an old man and he's going to be telling his grandchildren, 'When I was a little boy, this is what I did with my family.'"

Though Ray was raised attending a Christian church that preached that giving up the Native way of life was necessary for man, he is convinced of the opposite. He understands that returning to the Native way of life is critical for the survival of the planet, and therefore the survival of humans. Thankfully, he retained a lot of memories of Native philosophy from time spent with his elders.

"When we used to fish, we just had one little rowboat. When that one skiff was full, even if it was early in the morning, my grandmother would say, 'That's good; we're going in.' If I complained that there was still a lot of fishing that could be done, she said, 'You never, ever want to take more than what you need. You take what you need and leave the rest, and they'll be there for you tomorrow.' That was part of the circle of life philosophy of Indigenous people. We had to be really respectful of resources."

Being made costewards of Washington's fisheries as a result of the Boldt decision is a responsibility the tribe knows is necessary. Having seen commercial and sport fishermen with enormous traps set right at the mouth of rivers, they know that the decline of salmon is a direct result of overfishing and the destruction of the environment. Ray said, "One of the elders told me, 'You know, we used to have floods here and the color of the rivers wouldn't even change.' Now we have roads and clear-cuts and severe droughts and the first good rain we have, a flash flood will cover the salmon nesting beds with silt and destroy them. Things are really out of balance."

To get back in balance, he believes we have to recognize the spirit in all of life. "We're taught to see the spirit in plants, animals, birds, the water, and everything in and around us. We recognize too that there's one greater spirit that put all of that here.

"That Indigenous philosophy is really going to be important if we're truly going to try to put things back into place. We can't continue to put Band-Aids on everything that's wounded. There's only a certain amount that the earth can give; we can't take, and take, and take. We have to live in harmony with the spirit of the earth."

Ray glanced over at the picture on his office wall, of the time he looked a wild orca in the eye. In the boat were four generations of his family. If ancient Native philosophy holds true, each one of them gained spiritual power that day. It's up to the individual how that power is used, but perhaps Tsu'xiit wished for it to be channeled to tell a story: the story of how, as a species, we can do better. And to remember that, in Ray's words, "what happens to them will happen to us."

Learn more about the Tulalip Tribes and their environmental preservation efforts at www.tulaliptribes-nsn.gov.

CONCLUSION: The Interconnectedness of All Things

As kings and queens of the ocean, orcas are symbolic of the health of more than 70 percent of the surface of our planet—or about 97 percent of the earth's water. If a species that has no predators other than man can't survive, how long will it be before man can't survive? We would be wise to observe a species that has managed to exist on our planet for over 6 million years and take note of how it's managed to do so.

One obvious example we could adopt is the orcas' awareness and discipline when it comes to conservative consumption; they know enough to eat only 10 percent of the available food supply so that the supply does not collapse. There's no need to reinvent the wheel—if such a system works for ocean-based societies, why wouldn't it work for land-based societies? Even without observing this practice in other species, common sense tells us that overexhausting resources spells devastation in the end. So why do we keep doing it?

Human nature seems to be driven by the attitude of "Look what we can do!" We like creating problems so that we can use our technology to fix them. But never, ever can a man-made creation compete with what nature does when left alone. Nature knows that everything is interconnected, and no matter how intelligent we like to believe we are, the human mind does not have access to all the pieces.

Perhaps, like whales, we need to evolve from strictly a logic-based mentality to an existence that emphasizes emotion, intuition, and empathy. And we need to accept that we can't solve problems by going against nature or we will only introduce new ones. Finally, to know what it takes to move toward a more sustainable planet, we need to start at the top of the food chain.

A narrative video shared by Sustainable Human (a global community of collaborative video and content creators aimed to educate and bring awareness to the most important issues of our time) called "How Whales Change Climate" does an excellent job of representing the interconnectedness of all things—and the dependence our ecosystem has on whales. The narrator explains how when whales release their excrement, they discharge material from a diet of bottom-feeding fish that is rich in iron and nitrogen—elements that are scarce in surface waters. These elements fertilize plant plankton near the surface—which are kept near the surface by whales as they dive, and therefore given more time to reproduce.

This plant plankton goes on to feed the fish that the whales feed on—in other words, more whales equals more fish equals more whales, and so on. But whales and fish are not the only entities that benefit from this relationship; plant plankton also absorbs carbon dioxide from the atmosphere. As the plankton sinks, that carbon dioxide is brought to the bottom of the ocean and taken out of circulation for thousands of years.

Could the increased temperatures of our oceans be at least partially the result of a decrease in the ocean's number of whales? The video states that when whales were at their original numbers, they might have been responsible for removing tens of millions of tons of carbon from the atmosphere every year. It is suggested that one way to undo the amount of damage our species has done to the oceans and the atmosphere could be to allow whales to recover.

What Next?

There are enough dire conditions on our planet—several of which are outlined in this book—to make even an eternal optimist want to throw in the towel. But lest this background information leave you feeling hopeless, consider how many people are becoming aware of the implications of our environmental practices. If you're only noticing the negative, you're hanging out with the wrong people (and probably paying too much attention to the media).

Topics such as climate change—which was once a fringe topic—are becoming mainstream. There is Indigenous pushback and reclamation of tribal culture, pride, and practices—ones that are based on a healthier, spirit-led relationship between humans and nature. Like Native peoples, nature is starting to fight back after being beaten down for centuries. Sometimes it takes "crisis mode" for people to wake up and act.

This book chronicles only twenty-two action-driven individuals, but there are hundreds of thousands of people on this planet who are pioneering a brighter future for our planet, our oceans, and our cetaceans. It's easy to applaud and appreciate these people and move on with our lives, but the earth needs your participation too.

What do you care about? What feeds your soul? Maybe it's whales; maybe it's not...but the actions you take in your daily life affect them and the future of all life on earth, nonetheless. If the apex predators of the ocean come to find this planet inhabitable, it must be understood that there is little hope left for us. Perhaps that is why Native peoples consider whales to be our guides. If we can save them, we know we can save ourselves.

RESOURCES

FILMS

Blackfish
http://www.blackfishmovie.com/

Voiceless
https://bluefreedom.org/#film

The Cove
http://behindthecove.com/index_en.html

Sonic Sea
https://www.sonicsea.org/film

Jean-Michel Cousteau's *The Gray Whale Obstacle Course*
http://www.pbs.org/kqed/oceanadventures/episodes/whales

Chasing Coral
https://www.chasingcoral.com

BOOKS
War of the Whales: A True Story, by Joshua Horwitz

Whales of the West Coast, by David Spalding

Of Orcas and Men: What Killer Whales Can Teach Us, by David Neiwert

Inside Passage: Living with Killer Whales, Bald Eagles, and Kwakiutl Indians, by Michael Modzelewski

Eye of the Whale: Epic Passage from Baja to Siberia, by Dick Russell

Listening to Whales: What the Orcas Have Taught Us, by Alexandra Morton

Sightings: The Gray Whales' Mysterious Journey, by Brenda Peterson and Linda Hogan

Upstream: *Searching for Wild Salmon, from River to Table*, by Langdon Cook

Into Great Silence: A Memoir of Discovery and Loss Among Vanishing Orcas, by Eva Saulitis

ONLINE ARTICLES

"Going Aquatic: Cetacean Evolution," 2012, http://www.pbs.org/wnet/nature/ocean-giants-going-aquatic-cetacean-evolution/7577/

"How Long Have Humans Been on Earth," 2015, https://www.universetoday.com/38125/how-long-have-humans-been-on-earth/

"Are Whales Smarter Than We Are?" 2008, https://blogs.scientificamerican.com/news-blog/are-whales-smarter-than-we-are/

"Differences Between Baleen and Toothed Whales," 2018, https://www.thoughtco.com/baleen-vs-toothed-whales-3876141

"How Do Whales Breathe?" 2018, http://www.whalefacts.org/how-do-whales-breathe/

"Why These Whales Are 'Standing' in the Ocean," 2017, https://www.nationalgeographic.com/photography/proof/2017/07/sperm-whales-nap-sleeping-photography-spd/

"How Do Whales Communicate?" http://www.whalefacts.org/how-do-whales-communicate/

"Puget Sound Orcas Circle Ferry Carrying Artifacts," 2013, https://www.seattletimes.com/seattle-news/puget-sound-orcas-circle-ferry-carrying-artifacts/

"The Legend of Old Tom and the Gruesome 'Law of the Tongue,'" 2014, https://blogs.scientificamerican.com/running-ponies/the-legend-of-old-tom-and-the-gruesome-law-of-the-tongue/

"Humpback Whale Facts," http://www.whalefacts.org/humpback-whale-facts/

"Female Whales Forge Long-Lasting Friendships," 2010, https://www.livescience.com/6548-female-whales-forge-long-lasting-friendships.html

"Why Humpback Whales Protect Other Animals from Killer Whales," 2016, https://news.nationalgeographic.com/2016/08/humpback-whales-save-animals-killer-whales-explained/

"Whale Allegedly Protects Diver from Shark, but Questions Remain," 2018, https://news.nationalgeographic.com/2018/01/whale-protects-diver-from-shark-video-spd/

"Gray Whale," http://www.marinemammalcenter.org/education/marine-mammal-information/cetaceans/gray-whale.html

"A Gray Whale Migrated Nearly 14,000 Miles, Setting Record,"
2015, https://www.washingtonpost.com/news/morning-
mix/wp/2015/04/15/a-gray-whale-migrated-nearly-14000-miles-
setting-new-record/?noredirect=on&utm_term=.2070e9cdcaf9

"Big and Brilliant: Complex Whale Behavior Tied to Brain Size,"
2017, https://www.reuters.com/article/us-science-whales/big-
and-brilliant-complex-whale-behavior-tied-to-brain-size-
idUSKBN1CL30I

"Neuroanatomy of the Killer Whale (*Orcinas orca*) from Magnetic
Resonance Images," 2004,
https://onlinelibrary.wiley.com/doi/full/10.1002/ar.a.20075

"Danger: Dolphin Meat is Poisoned by Mercury,"
https://dolphinproject.com/campaigns/save-japan-
dolphins/danger-dolphin-meat-is-poisoned-by-mercury/

"December 12, 2003: Keiko's Life Has Ended,"
http://www.orcanetwork.org/Main/index.php?categories_file=Ke
ikos%20Story

"A Fight for Orca's Freedom," 2008,
https://www.seattletimes.com/seattle-news/a-fight-for-orcas-
freedom/

 "A Whale Is Found Dead with More Than 30 Plastic Bags in Its
Stomach—And Experts Say It's 'Not Surprising," 2017,
http://www.dailymail.co.uk/sciencetech/article-4185038/A-
whale-30-PLASTIC-BAGS-stomach.html

"Rock Stacking, Or 'Natural Graffitti [sic],' and Its Ecological
Impact," 2018, http://www.wideopenspaces.com/rock-stacking-
natural-graffitti-ecological-impact/

"Exxon Valdez Oil Spill Devasted Killer Whales," 2016, https://news.nationalgeographic.com/2016/01/160126-Exxon-Valdez-oil-spill-killer-whales-Chugach-transients/

"You Won't Believe How Japan Is Spending Extra Fukushima Relief Money," 2011, http://www.businessinsider.com/japan-fukushima-whale-meat-2011-12

"Fact Check: How Does Japan Compare with Other Whaling Nations," 2015, http://www.abc.net.au/news/2014-04-08/whaling-around-the-world-how-japans-catch-compares/5361954

"Cleaning Up Our Ocean," 2009, http://www.livingoceans.org/sites/default/files/reports/pollution_report.pdf

"NOAA Says Vessel Rules Are a Win for Orcas and Whale Watch Boaters," 2018, http://www.sanjuanjournal.com/news/federal-vessel-rules-are-a-win-for-orcas-and-whale-watch-boaters/

"Vessel Traffic Backgrounder," http://georgiastrait.org/wp-content/uploads/2015/03/231013-Vessel-traffic-backgrounder.pdf

"Navy Admits Sonar Killed Whales," 2002, http://www.sciencemag.org/news/2002/01/navy-admits-sonar-killed-whales

"Why We Pretend to Clean Up Oil Spills," 2016, https://www.smithsonianmag.com/science-nature/oil-spill-cleanup-illusion-180959783/

CONTRIBUTOR AFFILIATIONS AND ORGANIZATIONS MENTIONED

Whale, Sea Life and Shark Museum and Whale Research EcoExcursions
 www.oregonwhales.com

Oregon State Parks Whale Watching Spoken Here
https://oregonstateparks.org/index.cfm?do=thingstodo.dsp_whalewatching

Whale and Dolphin Wisdom Retreats
www.whaleanddolphinwisdomretreats.com

World Cetacean Alliance
http://worldcetaceanalliance.org

Orca Network
www.orcanetwork.org

Whale and Dolphin Conservation
http://us.whales.org

Samish Nation
www.samishtribe.nsn.us

Blue Freedom
www.bluefreedom.org

Orca Rescues Foundation
www.orcarescues.org

Aegean Marine Life Sanctuary
http://archipelago.gr/en/

Lime Kiln Point State Park and the Lime Kiln Lighthouse
www.parks.state.wa.us/540/Lime-Kiln-Point

The Whale Museum

www.whalemuseum.org

Sound Water Stewards
www.soundwaterstewards.org

University of Washington's COASST program
www.depts.washington.edu/coasst

Quileute Nation
www.quileutenation.org

Peggy Oki Art, Activism, and Public Speaking
www.peggyoki.com

Hannah Fraser Underwater Modeling and Performance Art
www.hannahmermaid.com

Surfers for Cetaceans
www.s4cglobal.org

Odin Lonning Artwork and Cultural Presentations
www.odinlonning.com

Sonar and Cetacean Mitigation Effort
www.facebook.com/sonarmitigation

North Gulf Oceanic Society
www.whalesalaska.org

Penn Cover Water Festival
www.penncovewaterfestival.com

Tulalip Tribes
www.tulaliptribes-nsn.gov

NONPROFIT ORGANIZATIONS TO SUPPORT

Center for Whale Research
https://www.whaleresearch.com

Orca Network
www.orcanetwork.org

DamSense
http://damsense.org

Orca Rescues Foundation
www.orcarescues.org

Aegean Marine Life Sanctuary
http://archipelago.gr/en/

Blue Freedom
www.bluefreedom.org

Whale and Dolphin Conservation
http://us.whales.org

The Whale Museum
www.whalemuseum.org

Save our Wild Salmon
http://www.wildsalmon.org

Wild Salmon Center
https://www.wildsalmoncenter.org

SHORE-BASED WHALE WATCHING ON THE WEST COAST

Lime Kiln Point State Park

www.parks.state.wa.us/540/Lime-Kiln-Point

West Coast Whale Watching Sites
http://whaleaware.org/index.php?page=whale-watching-from-land

The Whale Trail
https://thewhaletrail.org

RESPONSIBLE WHALE WATCHING COMPANIES

Visit the Pacific Whale Watch Association (PWWA) website (www.pacificwhalewatchassociation.com/) to find a whale watching company that fits your needs. The PWWA is proactive in coming up with safe boating guidelines around whales, some of which have now become regulations.

The Whale Heritage Sites (WHS) (http://whaleheritagesites.org) initiative is an accreditation scheme established by the World Cetacean Alliance (WCA). WHS are outstanding locations where cetaceans (whales, dolphins, and porpoises) are embraced through the cultural, economic, social, and political lives of associated communities and where people and cetaceans coexist in an authentic and respectful way.

Baja Ecotours
https://www.bajaecotours.com

Laguna San Ignacio Ecosystem Science Program
https://www.sanignaciograywhales.org/

Baja Discovery
http://www.bajadiscovery.com

CREDITS

Cover design by Antonio Garcia Martin
www.thisisagm.com

Cover image of map courtesy of The New York Public Library
https://digitalcollections.nypl.org/items/510d47da-f0b3-a3d9-e040-e00a18064a99

ECO-FRIENDLY LIFESTYLE TIPS

- ✓ Use canvas bags when shopping
- ✓ Buy in bulk using cloth bags and transfer the products to your own reusable containers
- ✓ Eat less meat (and don't buy farmed salmon!)
- ✓ Use compact fluorescent lamp or LED lightbulbs
- ✓ Use less paper (don't print unless absolutely necessary!)
- ✓ Use cloth napkins instead of paper towels
- ✓ Don't buy bottled water – carry a bottle with you wherever you go!
- ✓ Use only eco-friendly cleaners and creams (shampoos, soaps, lotions, etc.)
- ✓ Compost food scraps and eat organic as much as possible
- ✓ Plant a bird and bee-friendly garden
- ✓ Don't use chemical fertilizers on your lawn and garden – go organic!
- ✓ Plant native plants in your yard (this lowers watering requirements)
- ✓ Water house plants with leftover or unused water from drinking, cooking, and showering
- ✓ When ordering food, avoid receiving any unnecessary plastic utensils and straws by asking in advance
- ✓ Don't accept "free" promotional plastic products
- ✓ Simplify your life by only keeping belongings you use on a regular basis—donate the rest
- ✓ Reduce your purchases, and purchase used when possible
- ✓ Before making a purchase, ask yourself: Do I really need it? How did the production of this product impact the environment, and how will the disposal of this product (and any packaging material) impact the environment?
- ✓ When your current supply of disposable products (razors, food storage containers, batteries, ink cartridges, coffee filters, etc.) has been used, replace with reusable products
- ✓ Stop the delivery of junk mail to your address and switch all of your bills to paperless

Made in the USA
Columbia, SC
27 May 2018